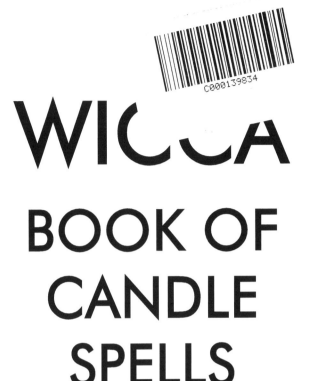

WICCA

BOOK OF CANDLE SPELLS

A Beginner's Book of Shadows for Wiccans, Witches, and Other Practitioners of Candle Magic

LISA CHAMBERLAIN

Wicca Book of Candle Spells

Published by **Chamberlain Publications (Wicca Shorts)**

ISBN-13: 978-1-912715-02-2

Disclaimer

YOUR FREE GIFT

Thank you for adding this book to your Wiccan library! To show my appreciation, I'm giving away an exclusive, free eBook to my readers—*Wicca: Little Book of Spells*.

The book is ideal for anyone looking to try their hand at practicing magic. The ten beginner-friendly spells can help you to create a positive atmosphere within your home, protect yourself from negativity, and attract love, health, and prosperity.

You can download it by visiting:

www.wiccaliving.com/bonus

I hope you enjoy it!

LEARN ABOUT WICCA
ON THE GO

Want to learn about Wicca during your morning commute, or while doing your household chores? These days it can be difficult to find the time to sit down with a good book, which is why I'm thrilled to announce that all of my books are now available in audiobook format!

Best of all, you can **get the audiobook version of this book or any other book by Lisa Chamberlain for free** as part of a 30-day Audible trial. Members receive free audiobooks every month, as well as exclusive discounts. It's a great way to experiment and see if audiobook learning works for you.

If you're not satisfied, you can cancel anytime within the trial period. You won't be charged, and you can still keep your book!

To choose your free audiobook from over 20 books about Wicca and related topics, including best-sellers *Wicca for Beginners* and *Wicca Book of Spells*, simply visit:

www.wiccaliving.com/free-audiobook

Happy Listening!

CONTENTS

INTRODUCTION

Welcome to my *Book of Candle Spells!*

Candle magic brings together two powerful sources of magical energy: the Element of Fire and the potent vibrations of color magic. Candle magic is widely recognized as the easiest form of magic for beginners to work with, as it is quite accessible and highly effective. Of course, seasoned magicians also still find candle spells rewarding, and this book is designed to bring new ideas to your magical practice no matter your level of experience.

Candles take center stage to varying degrees across this collection—some are focused exclusively on the combined magic of candle and color, while others incorporate additional tools such as crystals and other color-oriented ingredients. The spells are organized by color, and feature the 14 colors most widely used in Wiccan and other contemporary magic. You can personalize the spells by choosing your own preferred shades of any given color, if you like.

The spells in this book call for a variety of candle types. Many use spell candles, which are well-sized for single-use workings and available in Wiccan and occult-oriented shops, as well as online. Other spells call for pillar candles, which are longer-lasting and tend to be safer and sturdier than other candles. Tea lights and votives are easy to handle and work well in spells calling for multiple candles and outdoor workings.

Occasionally, a spell will call for a taper candle, which can be messy in terms of dripping wax, but this can be a nice enhancement of the magical atmosphere desired for spellwork. Many spells will call for "work candles," which are simply used to bring the mind into a more magical focus as the spellwork begins. These can be any size, and are always an option in any working, but are noted in the ingredients lists here when they're particularly helpful.

Some candle colors are more widely available than others, and depending on your access to magical supply shops, it might be more difficult to find certain colors. If need be, a white candle can be substituted for these colors, as will be discussed in the White chapter.

Many people wonder what to do with the unused portions of their candles after the spellwork is complete. Several spells call for letting the candle burn out on its own, but if you are instructed to extinguish the candle, you may use it again for atmosphere (just don't use it for other workings).

On occasion, disposal of the candle may be called for, if the working is for removal of negative energy. Traditionally, this is done by burying the candle, although some ecologically-minded Witches prefer not to disturb any life within the soil with a human-made object. This is entirely up to you, so do what your intuition advises. If you do choose to throw candle remnants in the trash, do so with an attitude of ceremony, rather than mindlessly tossing your magical leftovers in the bin.

When it comes to extinguishing candles, this is ideally done with a candle snuffer or by waving your hands over the flame, rather than blowing it out. If you do need to blow it out, just make a point of thanking the Element of Fire for its role in the spell before doing to. As for what to light your candles with, opinions abound on whether matches or a lighter is better for magical work. Use your intuition (or whatever you happen to have on hand!) in this regard as well.

Anointing candles with magically-charged oils is a time-honored tradition in Witchcraft, and many spells in this book call for the use of essential oils for this purpose. Most will offer a few different choices of oils, based on their magical correspondences. You are free, of course, to create your own blend using a combination of these and/or other oils, or use a tried-and-true blend you already work with, if it's sufficiently related to the purpose of the spell.

Do be aware of the amount of oil on your fingertips before lighting the candle, as oil is flammable! Wash or wipe your hands after anointing, if necessary. You can find more information about anointing candles and working magic with essential oils in my books *Candle Magic* and *Essential Oils Magic*.

As always, each spell in this book assumes that you have already energetically cleared and charged all ingredients prior to beginning the work. Charging candles can be as easy as holding them between your palms and sending your focused energy into the wax, or placing them on a consecrated pentacle slab. Depending on your practice, you might invoke the Goddess and God, the Elements, or other spiritual energies you work with to aid you in your magic. If you haven't yet learned to charge magical items, research and try a few different methods until you find what feels most appropriate for you.

Each spell also assumes you have done your part to bring yourself into a magically-focused state of mind, as this is the most important aspect of the work. This is a highly individualized process for each practitioner, but usually involves some kind of meditation or other relaxation technique. Many of these spells include reminders to spend time quieting your mind, but it's up to you to take this step before any magical working. It is ultimately *your* energy that's shifting the reality of the Universe, so shape it well and use it wisely!

Finally, while the words provided in these spells are effective at sealing the work, they are meant to be taken as suggestions only. If they resonate with you, then by all means use them! However, please feel free to substitute words of your own choosing, as this adds an extra element of your own unique magical power to the work.

It is my hope that you find many inspiring and useful spells among this candle-oriented collection. As always, remember that you are the magician, and any additions, subtractions, or other alterations to the spells that occur to you are worth trying, as long as they resonate with your own inner guide. Enjoy your continuing exploration of the world of candle and color magic!

Blessed Be.

RED

We all know red as the first color of the rainbow, but it is also among the most potent colors used in magic. It is not by any means a "neutral" color, and can provoke strong impressions, both positive and negative, depending on its context.

On the one hand, red roses are symbolic of love and passion, and are generally thought to be pleasing by those who give and receive them. On the other hand, the phrase "seeing red" describes feelings of anger and rage. Red is not a subtle color, to say the least!

At the most basic physical level, red relates to survival. It is the color of blood and of a healthy human heart. Red is also associated with the root chakra, which relates to issues of instinct, safety, survival, and boundaries. As such, red is associated with vitality and strength, good health, and the will to do what is necessary to survive and thrive.

This color is appropriate for magic related to physical healing and raising one's physical energy, as well as to motivation, willpower, ambition, and determination. Anything that contributes to basic security, such as business deals, career goals, or the acquisition of a home can benefit from red's magical energies. Red can also assist with issues requiring courage, fast action, leadership, and strength. It helps with confidence and self-esteem, and can help increase your personal vibrancy so that you stand out in a group.

Red's very masculine energy can be harnessed for workings related to lust and male sexual potency, as well as matters involving conflict or competition. Yet this color is also associated with the energies of joy, birth, celebration and renewal. And of course, red is the quintessential color of passion—whether related to romance, sex, a favorite hobby or pursuit, a social cause, or anything else you feel passionate about.

Red candles can add a "quickening" power to spellwork in general, but are particularly potent in spellwork related to any of the matters listed above. Red is a color of Fire and can be used in ritual to represent this Element. Astrologically, red is associated with the signs of Aries and Scorpio and the planet Mars. Its cardinal direction is South.

The spells in this chapter are aimed at helping you attract a passionate lover into your life, boost your physical energy, improve your health, and fire up your willpower to complete a challenging task.

PASSIONATE RELATIONSHIP SPELL

When you're ready for a new lover, don't just cast a general "love spell" without taking some time to consider what you really want out of a relationship. Otherwise, your powerful magic may bring you more of the same types of people you've already moved on from.

So take some time to clearly define what it is you're looking for. You may want to prepare a list of qualities that you desire in a lover ahead of time, since you'll be writing and speaking about them during the spell.

Of course, a truly healthy, passionate relationship must involve self-esteem and self-appreciation in both partners, so you'll also be focusing on yourself in this spell. Spend some time affirming for yourself the positive qualities that you have to bring to a new relationship so that you have them clearly in mind as you begin the work.

You will need:

- 1 red spell candle
- Cinnamon, jasmine, or rose essential oil
- Crystal point, athame, or other ritual carving tool
- White paper
- Red pencil or marker
- Scissors
- Wax paper

Instructions:

Carve a heart shape or other symbol of love into the candle, and anoint it with the oil. Now light the candle, and allow the wax to begin melting.

Meanwhile, cut two heart shapes, about the size of your palms, out of the paper.

Using the red pencil or marker, take one of the hearts and write the most important qualities you seek in a romantic partner. On the other heart, write a list of qualities you have to offer to another.

Hold the hearts in your hands for a moment as you focus on bringing new love into your life.

Now, place the hearts so that they overlap each other on a sheet of wax paper. Speaking out loud, take turns listing the qualities written on each heart.

As you list each one, drip a few drops of wax onto the hearts to seal them together. When you have finished speaking and the hearts are sealed, say the following (or similar) words:

> *"Passionate hearts, passionate minds,*
> *Passionate souls, we now entwine.*
> *So let it be."*

Place the hearts on your altar or in a special space in your home. Allow the candle to burn out on its own.

SUNLIGHT RITUAL
FOR PHYSICAL ENERGY

This spell draws on the color red's connection to the Sun and the Element of Fire. The Sun is the source of virtually all energy on our planet. This makes it the most obvious source to work with when you need to boost your physical energy!

As you perform this ritual, know that thousands of others across the world and throughout the span of human history, are with you. Cultures around the world, from the Aztecs to the Hindus to the ancient Egyptians to many Native American cultures revere the Sun in some way. It is an ageless tradition, offered here with a modern approach.

Ideally, this ritual is performed outside in direct sunlight on flat ground. However, you can create a vivid visualization of the Sun if you feel the need to work on a cloudy day, or work with bright lamplight and/or several large candles. All additional candles should be either red, yellow, orange, white, or pink.

You will need:

- 3 red candles
- Sunshine
- Work candle(s) for atmosphere (if working without direct sunlight)
- 3 large squares of tinfoil

Instructions:

Before the ritual, place one red candle (in a safe, sturdy holder) on each piece of tin foil. Arrange them on flat ground in a triangle shape, with enough space to stand in the center of the triangle.

Step inside the triangle and light the candles. Focus on the light of the candles and the sunlight bouncing off of the foil. Close your eyes, place your palms upward, and feel the warmth of the Sun on your skin.

With your eyes still closed, visualize the power of the Sun and the light of the candles filling your body with positive energy. See it start at your toes and work its way up until it reaches the top of your head.

Open your eyes and take a moment to feel the fullness of the solar energy inside of you. Say a word or two of thanks to the Sun for its never-ending energy and sustaining light.

Extinguish the candles and recycle the foil or save to use again when you repeat the ritual.

HEALING FIRE REGENERATION SPELL

Fire magic is excellent for banishing, and red's association with both Fire and health makes it the perfect choice for ridding yourself of a health issue. This spell honors the role of Fire in the forest—the destruction of the old in order to make room for the new. You will be "burning away" an old, unwanted physical form in order to bring in the new, healed, version of yourself.

Bay leaves are associated with healing and the fulfillment of wishes. What's more, burning a bay leaf in the home has been shown to relieve anxiety and boost the immune system!

As with any magic, this spell is not meant to replace needed medical care. However, it will certainly add power to any healing process initiated by a medical professional. And while your health issue may not be resolved overnight, you will be aligning yourself with healing vibrational frequencies, allowing the process to unfold at a much faster rate than it would otherwise.

Depending on the size of your bay leaf and fireproof bowl, you may want to keep a small amount of water on hand just to be on the safe side. If you don't have a red pencil, a regular pencil is fine.

You will need:

- 1 red spell candle
- 1 bay leaf
- 1 red pencil
- Small fireproof bowl
- Small cup of water (optional)

Instructions:

Before you begin, take three deep breaths and focus your energy on a white light radiating from your heart center. During each exhale, feel the light washing away any negativity or anxiety and allow your muscles to relax. When you feel calm, clear, and focused, light the red candle.

On the bay leaf, write down the health issue you're seeking to banish. Then spend a few minutes visualizing your body as you wish it to be.

For example, if you have an injured knee, visualize walking, running, jumping, etc. with two completely healthy and pain-free knees. If you have a cold, visualize breathing freely and having plenty of energy. Hold and strengthen this vision for a few moments.

When you feel ready, say the following (or similar) words:

"I release all imbalances of body, mind, and soul.
This fire of regeneration makes me whole.
It is done."

Now light the bay leaf on fire with the candle flame, and drop it into the dish to burn completely. (If the fire goes out before the leaf has completely burned, you can carefully relight it, either with the candle flame or a match.)

Allow the candle to burn out on its own. Scatter the ashes of the bay leaf over the Earth.

WILL-POWERED
VICTORY CHARM

Whether you're trying to incorporate a new exercise routine, give up an unwanted habit, clean out your basement, or conquer some other daunting task, the fiery energy of red will help you summon the will to get started and the drive to succeed.

Red jasper, a mineral stone revered for its grounding and strengthening properties, makes an excellent magical charm for this purpose, but you can use any red stone if need be.

You will need:

- 1 red pillar candle
- Crystal point, athame, or other ritual carving tool
- 1 piece of red jasper or other red stone
- Anointing oil (optional)

Instructions:

Carve a symbol appropriate to your goal into the candle. This can be a "V" for victory, a runic symbol with a similar meaning, a pentacle, or even your initials—whatever symbol holds power for you related to this particular magical goal.

Anoint the candle with the oil, if using.

Now hold the red jasper or other stone between your palms.

Close your eyes, take a deep breath, and envision yourself succeeding at your task. Enjoy the feeling of victory and the pride of self-accomplishment.

When you feel ready, place the stone in front of the candle.

Light the candle as you say the following (or similar) words three times:

"I am energy. I am willpower. I am success. I am worthy."

When the candle has burned out on its own, your victory charm is charged and ready to assist you. Keep it with you whenever willpower is needed to accomplish your goal.

ORANGE

The upbeat energies of orange are a blend of red and yellow energies. The influence of red brings the properties of strength, stamina, vitality and ambition, while yellow contributes energies of cheerful encouragement, confidence, and optimism.

Orange is useful in magic related to both physical concerns, such as boosting energy and personal power, and concerns of the mind, such as acquiring needed information, improving memory, or summoning mental agility in a challenging situation. As a color of sunrise and sunset, orange is both powerful and peaceful, promoting balance and a sense of warmth and well-being. And like the popular fruit that bears its name, orange is sustaining and rejuvenating.

Orange is associated with the sacral chakra, which governs creativity, movement, change, and emotions. The vibrations of orange can dispel depression, grief, feelings of abandonment, and other negative emotional energies, and help manage strong emotions. Orange also promotes joy, kindness, happiness, sharing, and an eagerness to have fun. It aids with social communication, and the ability to adapt smoothly to sudden change.

Orange is a color of Fire and can be used in solar magic, but its yellow-based energy also links it to the Element of Air. Accordingly, its cardinal direction can be either South or East. Astrologically, orange is associated with the Sun, the planets Mercury and Mars, and the signs of Leo and Sagittarius.

Orange is also a color of the harvest, and can be used in spells to bring forth the positive results of your recent efforts, especially when related to careers, promotions, and business. Orange brings success in legal matters, especially related to investments and to selling property, such as a home. It is also used to call in new opportunities in any of these areas.

The spells below work with orange candles and other orange ingredients to assist with adapting to change, raising your vibration through self-encouragement, strengthening your sense of empowerment, and boosting your vitality.

SPELL FOR NAVIGATING SUDDEN CHANGE

Change is often startling and uncomfortable. This is true whether the change is positive, negative, expected, or unexpected. When it comes to unexpected change, however, it's very common to get thrown off-balance by the disruption it causes. Yet all change brings with it new possibilities for improved circumstances, no matter how counterintuitive that may seem at the time.

This spell can help you navigate the choppy waters of unexpected change by shifting your perspective on the situation and rebalancing your energy, opening you up to receive unexpected blessings.

You will need:

- 1 orange pillar candle
- Orange or bergamot essential oil
- Oil burner or diffuser
- Journal or writing paper

Instructions:

Heat the oil in the burner or diffuser and then spend a few moments breathing deeply to quiet your mind.

When you feel grounded and centered, light the pillar candle and begin to freewrite about the situation.

Start by identifying the change that has happened, and then write about what you liked about the way things were before.

Spend some time envisioning what positive developments are possible now that this change has occurred. You don't need to know *how* these developments might come about—simply open your mind to the potential that this sudden change has made possible.

For example, if you've just lost a job, imagine what new and better opportunities could be coming your way. If you had travel plans that have fallen through, imagine what you can do with the time and money that have just been freed up.

Be creative and intuitive with your freewriting, rather than logical or analytical. Write for at least fifteen minutes total. As you write, imagine the candle shining a bright orange light upon you and surrounding you in its energetic field.

When you're finished, fold up the pages you've written and place them next to the candle. As you do so, say the following (or similar) words:

"Winds of change are the breath of life.
I am grounded, centered, and ready for new blessings.
So let it be."

Place the candle in a special place in your home and know that you can light it whenever you need some extra support during this time of change.

When some time has passed and you've adjusted to the change, you may want to revisit your freewriting to see how you have shifted since working the spell.

ENCOURAGEMENT SPELL FOR CHALLENGING TIMES

When faced with a difficult situation, whether it's a challenging task, a tough life transition, or simply a garden-variety case of "the blues," the vibrational frequencies of orange can be immensely helpful to your ability to overcome negative emotions. This spell will help you bring in the support you need by affirming what you are currently doing, honoring the character traits you admire in yourself, and encouraging an optimistic outlook.

You should shoot for as many encouraging notes as you can, but use a minimum of seven. If you can't find orange sticky notes, white or yellow will work just as well.

Note: because you will be leaving paper in close proximity to a burning candle, it's best not to leave the spell candle unattended at all. If this isn't possible, then gently extinguish the spell candle when the work is finished, and feel free to relight it along with the pillar candle at a later stage.

You will need:

- 1 orange spell candle
- 1 orange pillar candle
- Bergamot essential oil (optional)
- Several (at least 7) orange sticky notes

Instructions:

Anoint the spell candle with the oil, if using. Light the pillar candle and take a few moments to quiet your mind. Allow for the possibility of positive thoughts to flow into your experience.

When you're ready, begin to write messages of encouragement to yourself, using one sticky note for each message. For best results, focus on three categories: giving support to where you are in this moment, honoring what makes you feel good about yourself, and affirming an optimistic viewpoint.

Some examples of words of encouragement are "I am exactly where I'm supposed to be," "I am a kind person," and "I always rise to meet my challenges."

Write as many as you can, but make sure you agree with each statement you're making. If seven is all you can manage, that's perfectly fine!

Arrange the messages around the orange spell candle in a circle, reading each one aloud before you place it down. Visualize the power of the words giving you a boost of encouragement.

When you feel your energy begin to lift, light the spell candle as you say the following (or similar) words:

> *"Every positive word I say*
> *brings more light and joy my way.*
> *And so it is."*

If you can, allow the spell candle to burn out on its own. Place the sticky notes in various spots around your home, your car, or wherever else you will see them often.

You can continue to relight the orange pillar candle (as well as the spell candle, if need be) whenever you would like to reactivate the encouraging vibrations.

EMPOWERING ORANGE BATH SPELL

Ritual baths are often used for purification, calming, and healing purposes, but you can also use bath magic to promote more masculine energies like confidence and ambition.

If you're facing a challenge or situation that has you feeling uneasy, try this vibration-shifting spell, using orange's dual energies of peace and strength to dispel negative feelings and help you tap into your personal power. This is a great spell to do the night before an exam, a difficult conversation with a coworker or employer, or any other situation where you need to be both sharp and composed.

You will need:

- 1 orange candle
- Other candles for atmosphere (optional)
- 1-2 tablespoons dried orange peels
- 3-7 drops orange essential oil

Instructions:

Run a warm bath to begin the ritual.

When the tub is full, add the orange essential oil and scatter the dried orange peels over the water. Light the orange candle and any other atmosphere candles, and turn off any artificial lighting.

Gently enter the bath and breathe deeply, allowing the scent of the orange oil to envelop you. Take a few deep breaths, focusing only on your inhalation and exhalation. Note the shift in your personal energy as you continue to relax.

Now imagine the situation or challenge you are wanting to be empowered for. See yourself speaking and acting in a manner that you are completely satisfied with. Summon whatever it is you want to feel about the situation once it has passed.

When you have a strong hold on the feeling, take a deep breath in, and visualize orange light suffusing your entire body. On the exhale, release your vision and all further thought on the matter.

Take some time to enjoy the rest of your bath, and when you're ready, emerge from the tub, dry off, and gently extinguish the candle(s).

JUICY SUNSHINE
VITALITY SPELL

We all know that orange juice is good for you, but like any food, the nutritional properties of an orange can be magnified and energized by adding in some magic!

If you've been feeling depleted of energy, or if you just want to try a fun experiment with kitchen witchery, grab some oranges and a knife (you can use your athame for this if you like) and get ready for a sunny boost of energy!

You may want to work this spell in your kitchen, as it can be a little messy for altar work, but this is entirely up to you.

You will need:

- 3 orange candles
- 3 oranges
- Knife
- Cup

Instructions:

Place the three candles a few inches apart on your altar or kitchen table, and place one orange in front of each candle.

Slice the first orange in half, and set the two halves back in front of the candle. Then light the candle as you say the following (or similar) words:

"I thank the Sun for its life-giving light."

Repeat this process with the other two oranges. When lighting the second candle, say:

"I thank the Sun for its loving warmth."

When lighting the third candle, say:

"I thank the Sun for its sustaining energy."

Then take the halves of the first orange and squeeze their juice into the cup, focusing on the power and energy of the orange collecting in your cup through the light of the candle flame. Repeat this with the other two oranges.

When you have squeezed all the juice out of the oranges, take a moment to hold the cup in your hands. Take a deep breath in, letting the refreshing scent and the bright candle light wash positive energy over you.

Each time you take a sip of the orange juice say an affirmation like "I am filled with physical and mental energy." When you've finished the juice, gently extinguish the candles and enjoy your increased vitality!

YELLOW

The cheerful, sunny energies of yellow are known for having instant vibration-raising effects on those who simply gaze at the color for a few moments.

Yellow is actually the brightest color on the spectrum, and its harmonious energy helps us move away from the lower vibrations of stress and sadness. Yellow helps us open our capacity to enjoy the present moment, making way to experience optimism, happiness, and joy.

Yellow is primarily associated with the functions of the intellect, and is used in magic relating to memory, concentration, focus, and general mental clarity. It is the ideal magical color for students, as it assists with not merely acquiring knowledge, but truly understanding the subject matter one is studying. Yellow can help dissolve mental blocks and even accelerate the learning process, which is handy whether you're taking a class, training for a new job, or simply taking up a new hobby.

As a color of the Air Element, yellow is also used in spellwork related to creative intelligence— imagination, inspiration, ingenuity, and new ideas—in both the arts and the business realm. Draw on the power of yellow when you feel stuck in a creative project or need to contribute original ideas to a group endeavor. If you're seeking improved communication with friends or colleagues, or want to enhance your skills of persuasion, yellow is the ideal magical ally. Yellow is also used in spellwork related to travel—especially air travel—as well as intuition, divination, astral projection, and communicating with beings in the spirit realm.

Yellow also boosts self-awareness, self-esteem, and confidence, and is associated with the solar chakra, which governs these qualities. It is used in spellwork related to healing, pleasure, flexibility, beauty, and friendship. Yellow is also associated with the Sun as well as the planet Mercury, and the signs of Taurus and Libra. Its cardinal direction is East. As a Sun color, it is good for spells and rituals that call specifically on solar energies or deities associated with the Sun.

The magical workings below include a scrying session using the color yellow, spellwork focused on enhancing communication and boosting your self-confidence, and a "study buddy" in the form of an enchanted yellow candle.

COLOR SCRYING RITUAL

Scrying is an ancient and versatile form of divination, using water, crystal balls, tea leaves, and even cloud forms to reveal images and information not normally available to the conscious mind. But it isn't an art that comes easily to everyone.

This fun method uses the interaction between water and color to allow for more readily-seen images to come through, which works well as a beginning scrying exercise. For best results, try this at night by candlelight!

Yellow's association with the Element of Air and with divination makes it a great color to work with here, both in terms of the water and the candle(s). You may wish to approach this ritual with a specific question in mind, or simply be open to whatever images and impressions come through.

The food coloring will eventually dissolve into the water, but if you begin with cold water, you should have plenty of time for scrying before this happens.

You will need:

- 1 yellow spell candle
- Anointing oil (optional)
- Work candles for atmosphere (optional)
- Small bowl
- Cup of cold water
- Yellow food coloring
- Journal or writing paper (optional)

Instructions:

Find a quiet place to sit where you will be able to gaze into the bowl of water, ideally with the yellow candle(s) directly behind the bowl.

Anoint the spell candle with the oil, if using. Light any atmosphere candles and then spend a few moments quieting your mind. You may wish to think of a specific question at this time, but it's not necessary.

When you feel ready, open your eyes and light the yellow candle. You can state your question at this time, or simply affirm that you're open to helpful communication from the invisible realms.

Now pour the cup of water into the small bowl.

Train your focus on the water, emptying your mind of any other thoughts. Hold the bottle of food coloring about a foot above the bowl and squeeze three drops into the water.

With a soft gaze and receptive state of mind, sit quietly and allow any impressions from the yellow swirls within the water to arise in your consciousness. You may want to occasionally give the water a brief, gentle swirl with your finger to create more movement.

Feel free to write down any images, ideas, revelations, etc. that come to you during this exercise.

When you're finished, or when the food coloring has dissolved into the water completely, gently extinguish the spell candle and pour the water down the sink.

CONFIDENT COMMUNICATION SPELL

Many Witches and other magical practitioners find themselves to be the "odd one out" in group settings, whether it's at work, at school, or even among social acquaintances. Sometimes the gap between what we know of the Universe and how it is perceived through the lenses of "Muggles" is so great that we're afraid to open our mouths, lest we say something "weird" and create an awkward moment.

While you may never be able to open up someone else's mind to the hidden, magical underpinnings of reality, you should still feel free to speak your mind about any topic from your own unique perspective.

Yellow's airy and cheerful frequencies make it a great color to work with in this regard, as it fosters clear communication and a sunny aura at the same time. Those in your social sphere will be able to hear your words in whatever way makes the most sense for them, without discomfort or confusion causing conflict between you.

Most importantly, you will feel confident and secure within yourself, and not worried about what anyone else thinks about what you're saying!

You will need:

- 3 yellow votives or tea lights
- Bergamot, cinnamon, clove, or lemon essential oil (optional)

Instructions:

Anoint the candles with the oil, if using.

Arrange the candles in a line on your altar or workspace. The candle to the left represents you, and the candle to the right represents your "audience," or the people you come into contact with in your daily life. The candle in the middle represents your communications to others.

Light the first candle and say the following (or similar) words:

"I am a sovereign being, in tune with the workings of the Universe."

Light the middle candle and say the following (or similar) words:

"I speak with clarity, honesty, and integrity in all of my interactions."

Now light the third candle and say the following (or similar) words:

"My words are heard by those with ears to hear, hearts to feel, and minds to understand."

Allow the candles to burn for at least an hour, or all the way out on their own.

If you like, you can repeat this spell for each social context you move through in your daily life: work, school, friends, family, etc.

MIRROR MAGIC FOR SELF-ESTEEM

Everyone experiences challenges in the self-esteem department from time to time. This spell is designed for anyone who wants to feel good about themselves on a regular basis. And if you struggle with self-esteem to the point that you don't like looking in the mirror, then this spell is definitely for you!

Yellow's bright, harmonious energies of self-awareness, confidence, and encouragement can help you retrain your mind away from negative, unhelpful thoughts about yourself and toward more healing, positive, productive thoughts instead.

A large mounted mirror is ideal for this working, but a smaller mirror will also work—it just needs to rest securely against something so that you can write on it.

<u>You will need:</u>

- 1 yellow votive or tea light
- Work candle(s) for atmosphere (optional)
- Mirror
- Yellow Expo or other erasable marker

<u>Instructions:</u>

Light any atmosphere candles, and place the yellow candle so that you can see its reflection in the mirror.

Close your eyes and spend a few moments breathing deeply and quieting your mind.

When you feel ready, light the yellow candle and look directly at yourself in the mirror. Using the yellow non-permanent marker, begin to write adjectives and phrases that describe all of your positive qualities.

For example, you could write words such as "friendly, caring, thoughtful, articulate, intelligent," etc. You can identify talents and skills that you're proud of, or even write about past accomplishments that you're still proud of. Be creative in assessing all of your best characteristics!

However, be sure that you believe these things about yourself, at least some of the time. In other words, if you feel your heart sinking as you write a word because you don't think it's true, then you're putting negative energy into the spell and severely reducing its effectiveness. So if you've always loved baseball, but truly aren't skilled at it, don't write "good at baseball." Instead, write something like "good at loving baseball!"

Cover the mirror with as many words and phrases as you can. When you're finished writing, take a moment to read the words you have written. Repeat them out loud as you look into your own eyes in the mirror.

Close your eyes and take a deep breath, internalizing the positive vibrations of the words and their yellow color. Exhale and open your eyes, gazing at yourself in the mirror a final time.

Leave the candle near the mirror to burn out on its own. You can leave the words up on your mirror to read each day, or take a photo of the work to print and place on your altar before wiping the mirror clean.

YELLOW
"STUDY BUDDY" SPELL

If you have an important test coming up, a class presentation in which you really need to shine, or even such a burdensome number of class assignments that you don't know where to start, try this creative, hands-on spell. Yellow's airy, intellectual energies will physically merge with the academic material you're working with and bring you into the ultimate "study flow."

Ideally this spell is worked with an actual textbook, folder, or binder that you use for your class, but if this isn't applicable, you can use any book or other study material as a representation of your task.

You will need:

- 1 yellow pillar candle
- Peppermint, clary sage, or bergamot essential oil
- Several feet of yellow ribbon
- Scissors
- Textbook or binder

Instructions:

Anoint the candle with the oil as you visualize yourself assimilating new information, sparking new ideas, and moving from task to task with ease.

Light the candle and allow the wax to melt for a while until a small pool has gathered. Meanwhile, wrap a piece of yellow ribbon vertically around the front cover of the textbook or binder.

When the wax is ready, cut the ribbon to overlap just a bit and seal the ends of the ribbon together by dripping a small bead of wax on one end. Repeat this with the back cover of the textbook or binder.

Hold the enchanted book or binder in your hands and say the following (or similar) words three times:

"My mind is sharp, focused, and ready. I learn with each new breath."

Now cut several 8-inch pieces of ribbon that you can then use as bookmarks or placeholders while you are studying.

Place the candle, bookmarks, and study materials in your study area and get to work!

GREEN

Green is a color widely associated with the season of spring and the bursting forth of new life. It is the color of grass, leaves, and plant life in general, and is used in magic associated with the fairy realm.

Containing the energies of both yellow and blue, this vibrant color is both healing and uplifting, and its masculine and feminine energies evoke a sense of balance and harmony. As the color of the heart chakra, green is a mediator between the realm of thought and the realm of emotion, and assists in workings related to compassion, love (including love of self) and healthy partnerships, including marriages.

In the magical world, green is perhaps best known as the color of abundance and good luck. In fact, it is the predominant color of paper money in the United States, which gave rise to the slang term "green" in reference to cash. Green is indeed used in spellwork related to increasing financial well-being, but it's also very effective for any kind of abundance, whether it's good health, supportive friends and family, or a farm or garden ripe with nourishing crops.

Green is also associated with the related concept of prosperity—a reliable, continuous source of well-being as opposed to a one-time boon of good fortune. As such, green is also excellent for workings related to employment or career matters, the growth of business, and positive returns on investments.

Green's association with the flourishing of plant life makes it an ideal color for spellwork focused on physical fertility, as well as all kinds of renewal, rebirth, rejuvenation, and transformation. It is a color of new beginnings, and can be used to support personal growth and progress toward any goal. Of course, green is highly appropriate for magic related to gardening, gaining skills in herbal healing, preservation of trees and other plant life, and environmental concerns.

Green is a color of Earth and can be used in magic and rituals to represent this Element. Astrologically, it is associated with the planets Venus, Jupiter, Mars, and Mercury, and with the signs of Aquarius, Cancer, and Taurus. Its cardinal direction is North.

The spells in this chapter utilize green candles to boost your financial prosperity, help you gain rewarding employment, increase chances of conceiving a child, and promote good luck.

MAGIC CASH SPELL

There are many spells out there that involve charging actual cash—either coins or paper bills—to attract more cash. This version draws very directly from the power of the green spell candle, with a little help from prosperous patchouli oil.

You will need:

- 1 green spell candle
- Patchouli essential oil
- 1 five-dollar bill
- Green rubber band

Instructions:

Anoint the candle with the patchouli oil.

Fold the five-dollar bill in half lengthwise and wrap it around the candle.

Secure the bill with the rubber band, leaving at least an inch of space between the bill and the candle wick so that the flame will not ignite the bill.

Now hold the wrapped candle between your palms and summon up the feeling of being flush with cash, with all of your basic needs met and the ability to spend some money on yourself!

When you have a solid hold on this feeling, say the following (or similar) words three times:

"As above, so below.
So money in my life does flow.
Land to sky, shore to shore,
this money brings me money more."

Light the candle and allow it to burn down to the top of the five-dollar bill.

Gently extinguish the candle, and when the wax has cooled, unwrap the bill.

Carry it with you in your wallet, but don't spend it—instead, whenever you see it, remind yourself that you are attracting more cash into your life each day.

LUCKY PENNY
EMPLOYMENT SPELL

Job hunting is one of those tasks where our personal energy makes all the difference—not just at the interview, but in every step leading up to it. Being confident that you will find a well-paying job that you actually like greatly increases your chances of manifesting this outcome.

This spell allows you to focus the positive energy of your grandest desires into a physical talisman that you can carry with you throughout the job-seeking process—including to that final interview!

If you're concerned about protecting the surface of your altar or work space from any spilled candle wax, you might want to place a small piece of wax paper under the coin.

You will need:

- 1 green spell candle
- Patchouli, clove, lavender, or bergamot essential oil
- 1 new penny
- Wax paper (optional)
- Journal or writing paper (optional)

Instructions:

Anoint both sides of the penny with the oil, and then place it face-up on your altar or table, in front of the spell candle.

Light the spell candle and, as the wax begins to melt, spend several minutes focusing on how you will feel once you're working in your new ideal job.

For extra powerful magic, freewrite for awhile on the characteristics of the job you wish to manifest.

When you feel a strong sense of satisfaction with your vision, and when enough wax has melted, carefully tip the candle to drip three drops of green wax onto the coin.

As you do so, say the following (or similar) words:

"The job is mine. It is done."

Return the candle to its holder and allow it to burn out on its own.

Once it's out, keep the coin with you in your pocket or purse as you go out and find your ideal new job.

CANDLELIGHT
FERTILITY SPELL

For women struggling to conceive a child, much assistance can be found from herbal medicine, acupuncture, and modern medical treatments. In conjunction with whatever you are currently trying, this simple spell can help create the vibrational atmosphere necessary for conception to occur.

Because fertility and conception are such personal undertakings, the symbol you carve into the candle should be chosen by you. If you aren't familiar with any fertility symbols, do some research (there are many, many options from cultures around the world to choose from) or create your own.

In preparation for this spell, be sure to take some time to quiet your mind, breathe deeply, and let go of any and all negative thoughts, especially related to the subject at hand.

This is important for any magical undertaking, but it's especially crucial when it comes to fertility, since your physical body is the literal location where the magic will manifest. Make sure that the energy you put into this work is coming from a relaxed, clear, and optimistic frame of mind.

You will need:

- 1 large green pillar candle
- Clary sage, ylang ylang, and/or geranium essential oil
- Symbol(s) of fertility
- Crystal point, athame, or other ritual carving tool

Instructions:

Carve your chosen fertility symbol into the candle. As you carve, visualize the joining of your life force with another to produce a new human being.

Anoint the candle with the oil, and then simply light the candle whenever you join with your mate.

Repeat the spell in the event that the candle has been spent before conception occurs.

SEVEN-DAY
LUCK BOOSTING SPELL

Since ancient times, different cultures have held different beliefs about "luck." Many believed that the positions of the stars and planets ruled one's luck, while others petitioned creatures such as fairies and sprites to bring them luck. But whatever the merits of these traditions may be, it has been shown time and time again that approaching life with a positive attitude and a spirit of hopefulness has the most direct impact on our "luckiness" in life.

This fun spell harnesses the traditional color of luck while helping you to develop a more deliberate practice of positive thinking in your daily life.

You will need:

- 7 green votive candles
- 7 small slips of paper
- Green pencil, pen, or marker
- Small bowl

Instructions:

To prepare for this spell, write seven positive affirmations, one on each slip of paper. You can use the examples provided below, or write your own.

Fold each slip after writing the affirmation, and place them all in the bowl.

Place the seven candles in a row on your table or altar.

On the first morning of the spell, right after you wake up, light a single green candle. Swirl the pieces of paper around in the bowl and choose one at random. Read the affirmation out loud, and tuck one end of the slip of paper carefully under the lit candle. After a few moments, or when it's time to leave the house, gently extinguish the candle.

On the second morning, light the first candle again and a new candle, so that you have two green candles lit. Re-read the affirmation from the first morning, and then choose a new affirmation from the bowl to read aloud today. Tuck the new affirmation under the new candle, and leave both candles burning for a few moments or until it's time to leave the house.

Repeat this process for a full seven days. You will be delightfully surprised at how much "luck" you are tapping into as you increase your positive vibrations over the course of the week!

Example positive affirmations:

It is no accident that I am here on this Earth.
A million untold things work out for me every single day.
I am an excellent manifestor of my dreams.
Unexpected miracles happen every day.
I am lucky enough to have discovered magic.
I am really enjoying this experiment called "life."
I am wide open to the very best of possibilities.

BLUE

As the color of the sky on a sunny day, which we also see reflected in bodies of water, blue is a peaceful color with soothing properties, much like the effect of gazing at the ocean or a calmly flowing river. Accordingly, it is often used magically to bring about peace, calm, tranquility, and patience, helping us learn to "go with the flow" of life's unexpected twists and turns.

Blue is useful for sleep issues, including insomnia and disturbing dreams, and resolving anxiety in the mind and body. A truly healing color, blue can be used in magical workings to examine and resolve difficult emotions, and promote feelings of stability.

Blue is the color of the throat chakra, which governs deep communication and the ability to be honest with ourselves and others. Difficult conversations can be facilitated with spellwork involving this color, as blue helps us discover and speak our inner truths, and understand previously hidden truths about seemingly complex situations.

Its ability to help release stuck emotions makes it a great color for spellwork related to weight loss. It is also used in spellwork for protection from disharmony and negative vibrations, especially related to the home, and to promote wisdom, confidence, justice, and good fortune. Blue can assist with strengthening relationships of all kinds by promoting loyalty, sincerity, faith, devotion, reliability, and trust.

Blue is also associated with spiritual matters, and is used in workings related to psychic ability, astral projection, prophetic dreams, and meditation. If you are looking to increase your connection to the spiritual realm, be sure to work with the energies of blue. Blue's

Elemental association is, of course, Water, and its cardinal direction is West. Astrologically, it is associated with the Moon, the planets Jupiter, Neptune, and Mercury, and the signs of Virgo, Capricorn, Aquarius and Pisces.

Below, you'll find spellwork for protecting your home from negative energies and facilitating harmony among its inhabitants, increasing your capacity for patience, and becoming your own emotional guide and healer.

BLUE PERIMETER HOME PROTECTION SPELL

The vibrations of well-being that emanate from the color blue makes it an ideal color for a protection spell against negative energy—whether the negativity comes in the form of your own thoughts, other nonphysical energies within the home, or other people.

The subtle energetic adjustment created by this spell can help you turn your home into a true sanctuary, where the most positive and healing aspects of yourself and others can flourish.

This spell requires some extra caution, as you will be leaving lit candles temporarily unattended while you move from room to room. Make sure to take any necessary precautions regarding pets and children beforehand.

For best results, it's good to straighten up, sweep, dust, and/or whatever might be needed to create a sense of calm and order in the house. You may also want to purify the energy by smudging with herbs, or another space-clearing method.

You will need:

- Blue tea lights or votives (enough for each door and window into your home)

- Small bag or basket to carry candles

Instructions:

Place all of the candles in the bag or basket and hold it in your arms.

Focus on harnessing the energy of protection and concentrating it into all of the candles.

When you're ready, starting with the front entrance, place a blue candle on the floor at the center of the door. Light the candle, and visualize a blue wall of vibrant light sealing off this area of your home from unwanted energies and visitors.

Moving clockwise around your house, repeat these steps at every window and any additional doors—every potential entrance to your home. (If you have a working chimney, place one at the hearth as well.)

When you have reached the front entrance again, take a deep breath and visualize your entire home surrounded by protective blue light, and say the following (or similar) words:

"All energy within these walls is positive, peaceful, and for the good of all. And so it is."

Leave all the candles burning simultaneously for at least three minutes while you enjoy the feeling of security and peace permeating your living space.

To close the ritual, start again with the front entrance and gently extinguish the candle. Work clockwise again through the house, extinguishing each flame.

You can reuse these candles for atmosphere, or whenever you'd like to summon a feeling of reassurance while in your home.

HARMONY SPELL
FOR DOMESTIC CONFLICTS

The Blue Perimeter Home Protection spell above is excellent for maintaining healthy and positive energy within your home. However, interpersonal conflicts among roommates or family members can still flare up and even persist over time. After all, we learn through our relationships, all of which are bound to have their thornier aspects at times.

This spell can facilitate that learning, and the resolution of the conflict, by providing a sacred space and time for honest and healing dialogue.

This spell is particularly effective because blue is the color of peace, and also because it requires that both parties be willing to work through and resolve a disagreement. (Note that it does require the willing physical participation of the other person involved.)

You will need:

- 1 blue pillar candle
- 2 pieces of blue or white yarn, long enough to wrap around the candle

Instructions:

You should sit facing one another with the candle placed between you, either at a table or on a raised platform, so that the candle is safe to handle once it's lit.

Take a moment to breathe and center yourself by visualizing a white light surrounding you both. Ask the other person to do the same, so that you both come to the ritual with healing intentions.

Light the candle and open an honest discussion about how to restore harmony in the home. Be frank, but respectful to one another. Practice using "I statements" (such as "I feel _____ when you _____" throughout the discussion.

47

It is important to avoid an attitude of blame or of right and wrong; rather, invite the person to work *with* you to solve the argument. This may take some time, so allow the space and time needed to truly clear the air and find resolution.

When you are each satisfied that you have been heard by the other and peace is restored, each person should carefully tie their piece of yarn around the candle to signify their commitment to keeping harmony in the home.

You can gently extinguish the candle at any point after this and relight it on each successive evening until the candle is spent.

SPELL FOR INCREASED PATIENCE

Whether you're experiencing frustrations at work, at home, within a relationship, or even simply with yourself, the healing properties of blue can assist you with releasing your pent-up negativity and harnessing patience in triggering situations.

This spell involves exploring your stress-based responses to the situation you need help with, and the creation of a talisman to help you move through future triggers with more grace and ease.

You will need:

- 1 blue spell candle
- Lavender, vetiver, palmarosa, and/or bergamot essential oil (optional)
- Journal or writing paper
- 1 blue adventurine, blue topaz, blue opal, or other blue mineral stone

Instructions:

Take a moment to relax and release the stress of the day. Breathe deeply and shift your focus from the world around you to the world inside you.

Anoint the candle with the oil, if using. Light the candle, and place the stone in front of it.

Begin freewriting about the relationship, job situation, family issue, etc. that has prompted you to work this spell.

Start by identifying the situation, and then write about how it makes you feel.

If you find yourself getting worked up about it as you write, try looking past your immediate reaction to what may be lying underneath the issue. Are there memories from your past trying to come up? Are there fears being activated by the current situation?

Write whatever comes to mind, and keep writing for at least 20 to 30 minutes.

When you feel clearer and more calm about the situation, take the blue stone and hold it between your palms. Visualize blue light radiating from within the stone and surrounding your entire body.

Hold this vision for a few moments, and when you're ready, say the following (or similar) words:

"Patience and peace,
ease and flow,
these old triggers I now let go.
So let it be."

Place the stone back in front of the candle and allow the candle to burn out on its own.

Carry the stone with you in your pocket or purse, and hold onto it whenever you experience a trigger that threatens your patience.

"LOVE NOTES TO SELF" MEDICINE SPELL

Encouragement and support from other people in our lives is a much-needed factor in healthy living. However, too much dependence on others creates imbalance, as we are ultimately each our own best friend, guide, and healer.

This spell is designed to provide you with the guidance and love of your higher self during times when you really need it, but might be less likely to be able to access these positive frequencies.

When worked with an appropriate amount of well-directed energy, this spell is incredibly powerful. This is because you're harnessing your most positive, peaceful, loving vibrations and storing them for when you need a lift out of more negative states like anxiety, despair, or just plain old energetic depletion.

Therefore, this is one of those workings that's best done well in advance of when you might actually benefit from it most. So the next time you find yourself on top of the world, take advantage of it and write yourself some magically charged "love notes"!

You will need:

- 1 blue candle
- Several small pieces of paper
- Blue pen, pencil, or marker
- Wax seal
- Small bowl

Instructions:

Take some time to quiet your mind, and then focus on the feelings of well-being that you are currently experiencing.

Light the candle, and begin to write yourself several positive "love notes" on the pieces of paper. Write as many as you can, with a minimum of at least seven.

For example, you might write "I love and appreciate who you are," or "I am so proud of all the work you have already done," or "You shine brightly, even when you don't know it!"

Fold each paper in thirds, overlapping so that the message is sealed inside.

By this point, the blue candle should have melted a good bit of wax. Drip a small amount of wax onto the fold of the paper and press the wax seal down to firmly secure it.

When the last note is sealed, gently extinguish the candle.

Keep these notes in a small bowl on your table or altar.

The next time you need some emotional TLC, take out a message from the bowl and read it! You may wish to keep the rest of the candle on hand for this purpose as well.

INDIGO

Associated with midnight skies and outer space, Indigo is perhaps the most mysterious color in the visible light spectrum. In fact, there has been much debate as to whether or not it actually even exists in what we think of as the rainbow.

Regardless, indigo is a color of intense spirituality, and is associated with the Akashic Records—the vast invisible realms where all information about every life ever lived can be accessed. As a blend of blue and violet, indigo contains properties of both colors, making it useful in magic related to healing, expression, spirituality, and esoteric insight.

Indigo is the color of the third eye, and helps bring forth inner knowledge from the subconscious. It is associated with the brow chakra (though violet plays this role in some systems), which governs perception, insight, clairvoyance, imagination, and dreams.

Use indigo's fluid energies for powerful results in workings related to psychic receptivity, intuition, and divination, as well as wisdom, sharpened perception, and discernment. Indigo facilitates deep meditative states, and guidance and healing on the spiritual level.

Indigo is also used in workings to aid with depression and improve focus, as well as balancing intense emotion with rational objectivity. It can be used to stop or counteract negative gossip and to slow down or halt an unwanted situation. In either of these cases, just be sure your focus is on the results you seek for yourself, rather than on manipulating others.

A color of dignity and self-mastery, indigo can help tame unwanted aspects of one's own character and support devotion to worthy people and causes in one's life. Indigo is associated with the planets Venus and Saturn, the signs of Gemini and Aquarius, and the Element of Air. Its cardinal direction is East.

The workings in this chapter utilize the special properties of indigo to help you get your own magical meditation practice going, increase your psychic receptivity, find clarity about a murky situation, and clear your physical body of unwanted energy.

INDIGO ZONE MEDITATION PRACTICE

It can be argued that all successful magic is worked in a meditative state—once the practitioner has successfully cleared their mind of all extraneous thoughts and concerns, making room for effective visualization of the magical goal. Yet many beginning Witches may struggle with this all-important step, since the mind pretty much always resists being quieted at first.

Getting into a regular meditation practice goes a long way toward boosting this aspect of your magic, and offers a range of physical, emotional, and mental benefits as well!

This ritual draws on the unique frequencies of indigo, and is designed to help you foster your own regular practice of getting in the "zone" for magic.

Be sure to make yourself as comfortable as you can—no need to sit cross-legged on the floor if that doesn't work for you. You can sit on pillows, in a chair, on the couch, etc. (You can even lie down, though if doing so will make you sleepy, then it's best to sit upright.)

You may also wish to play soft, simple music or other meditative sounds (such as Tibetan chimes) in the background. Try searching for free streaming ambient music online—you'll find plenty to choose from.

Just be sure that the sounds won't distract you—overly melodic or complex music tends not to be helpful. If you're in a place where noise is likely to interrupt you, try using earplugs for an easier time quieting your mind.

Finally, if you find that you need a more structured, guided mediation to get you in the flow, you can also find plenty of these online to listen to while the candle burns. Consider experimenting with a different guided meditation each day to see what works best for you.

<u>You will need:</u>

- 1 large indigo pillar candle
- Quiet, comfortable place to sit
- Timer
- Ambient/meditation music (optional)
- Earplugs (optional)

<u>Instructions:</u>

Light the candle and spend a few moments simply gazing softly at the flame. When you're ready to begin the meditation, set your timer for 5 minutes.

Now gently allow your eyes to close and take a slow, deep breath in through your nose.

Visualize the air flowing through your nose and down your throat, into your lungs. Then extend the breath into your heart center and down into your belly.

As you slowly release the breath, see it leaving your belly first, traveling back up through your heart center and your lungs, up through your throat and back out through your nose.

Repeat this breathing process three times.

Now allow yourself to breathe normally, keeping your attention on your inhale and exhale. When you find your mind wandering (and it almost certainly will), simply return your attention to your breath.

Be gentle and patient with your mind—you are asking it to do something it's unfamiliar with, and struggling or becoming frustrated will not help it quiet down.

Don't worry about how much or how often your mind wanders, since the mere act of trying to slow it down is benefiting you. Over time, with regular practice, meditation will become easier and more rewarding.

When the timer goes off, take a final deep, slow breath, gently open your eyes and extinguish the candle. You can reuse the candle for your subsequent meditations until it is spent.

Try this meditation for 5 minutes per day for three days, and then add a minute or two for the next three days. Gradually build up to at least 15 minutes per day, if you can.

Once you build this habit, getting into "the zone" for magic will be much easier!

INDIGO PSYCHIC RECEPTIVITY PRACTICE

This ritual can be used as a follow-up to the Indigo Zone Mediation Practice (above), or on its own. As a practice, it helps train the mind to enter a meditative state, but also opens you up specifically for messages from your subconscious to come through.

This is also a good "training" exercise for the Elemental Flame Communication exercise in the Violet chapter, below. Try it for a few days and see what kind of shifts occur in your awareness of the subtle energies within and outside of your mental space.

<u>You will need:</u>

- 1 indigo candle
- Small hand-held bell
- Journal or writing paper

<u>Instructions:</u>

Take a few deep, centering breaths to signal to your mind and body that it's time to turn inward, away from the distractions of the day.

Light the candle and ring the bell three times.

Let your gaze soften as you listen to the vibrations ripple ever outward, passing beyond your range of hearing and ultimately merging with all vibrations in the Universe.

As the sound of the bell fades, focus on the flame of the candle. Remain focused on the flame for as long as you can, but be sure to blink when you need to.

Whenever thoughts distract you from the flame, acknowledge them and then gently allow them leave your awareness. If you like, you can ring the bell again to recenter your focus. Stay in this meditative mode for at least 10 minutes.

Afterward, with the candle still burning, spend 10 to 15 minutes freewriting in your journal about anything that comes to mind.

You may write about thoughts that occurred to you during the mediation, any images you noticed in the candle flame, or simply whatever thoughts are flowing through your mind in the moment, however mundane they may seem.

After working this ritual a few times, reread your freewriting from each session and take note of any patterns that come up.

SPELL FOR CLARITY

Our analytical minds often don't want to leave a problem alone, even when we know we can't figure out a solution just yet. This can actually keep the problem around longer than it needs to be, as we keep it active in our vibrational frequencies through our thoughts about it. In these instances, clarity cannot arise until we have let go of the problem completely, at least for a moment.

This is a great spell for moving toward resolution of any kind of "muddy" situation—a decision to make, a seemingly intractable problem, or a vague sense of something being wrong that you can't quite identify. Rather than over-thinking and over-analyzing the question, you will be allowing your inner knowing to bring clarity to the situation. Indigo helps connect us to the etheric plane through our Third Eye (or pineal gland), bypassing the analytical mind to receive pure wisdom.

This spell can be worked on its own or in conjunction with the Indigo Zone Meditation Practice, above. (For best results, use a new indigo candle, in addition to your meditation candle, for this working.) You may also wish to use earplugs and/or ambient music to help you keep your focus.

You will need:

- 1 indigo tea light, votive, or spell candle
- Timer (optional)
- Journal or writing paper (optional)

Instructions:

To begin, identify your question or issue, and state it out loud as you light the candle. If you like, you can say the following (or similar) words:

*"From my subconscious mind, connected to All That Is, I call forth
clarity on _____."*

Spend a few moments simply gazing softly at the flame and breathing deeply. When you feel ready, close your eyes and touch the index and middle fingers of your dominant hand to the center of your forehead, just above your brows. This is the opening to your third eye, where your access to intuition and psychic visions resides.

Visualize the light of the candle floating into your conscious awareness, behind your closed eyelids. Hold this vision as long as possible, and simply relax into this meditative state. (If you like, set a timer at the start of the spell for at least 7 minutes.)

Don't think about your question—surrender it instead to the subconscious. If you find yourself getting distracted, gently return your focus to the flame at your third eye.

When you are finished, you can write down any messages or impressions that came to you during the ritual. However, don't expect the answer to your question to come right away—it may need to percolate in your subconscious for awhile until the time is right for you to receive the information.

Just go on about your day, and if your attention gets stuck back on the issue, remind yourself that it is being resolved behind the scenes, and that you will know what to do when the time is right.

SPIRITUAL CLEANSING BATH

If you've been feeling tired, stressed, anxious, or depressed with no obvious cause, it may be time to clear your body of old or unwanted energies.

The power of natural Himalayan salts is well-known for its detoxifying properties—not just on the physical level, but on the spiritual level as well. The energetic vibrations of indigo enhance the work by helping you achieve and maintain a calm, meditative state.

Note: if you have not worked with Himalayan salts before, it's advisable to start with a smaller amount, as its detoxifying effects can cause drowsiness or dizziness. Keep a glass of water to drink near the tub in case you begin to feel weak or sleepy.

You will need:

- 4 indigo candles
- ½ to 1 cup fine-grain Himalayan salt
- Bergamot, lavender, patchouli, and/or vetiver essential oils (optional)
- Drinking water (optional)

Instructions:

Begin by placing an indigo candle at each corner of your bathtub.

Run the water at a comfortable temperature.

Once the bottom of the tub is covered in water, pour in the salt. When the tub is full, light each of the candles with healing and clearing intentions.

Gently submerge yourself in the water and shed all of the stress of the day through focusing on your breathing. Allow your mind to clear.

When you are ready, visualize the light of the four candles uniting above you and entering your cleansed body to heal and refresh your spirit.

Stay in the tub for at least 20 minutes and up to 45 minutes.

When you are done, drain the bathtub and exit carefully. Gently extinguish the candles, and treat yourself to a relaxing evening as your body integrates the effects of the ritual bath.

VIOLET

A color found in delicate flowers as well as spectacular sunrises and sunsets, violet is the highest vibration of the colors in the visible spectrum. It contains the energies of both red and blue, with characteristics of each to be found in its magical purview.

The influence of red makes this color appropriate for workings related to power, success, and ambition, as well as increased enthusiasm for an endeavor. The blue aspects are excellent for magic connected with spirituality, wisdom, emotional healing and attaining hidden knowledge. Violet is also commonly referred to as "purple," and while there are technically distinctions between these two colors, they can be thought of as one and the same for the purposes of candle magic.

Those who work with the color indigo will notice a fair amount of overlap with violet when it comes to magical purposes, but there are some important distinctions. Where indigo's powers are primarily concerned with inner mysteries, violet is more about tuning into broader, universal energies.

Violet is associated with the crown chakra (although in some systems, the color white plays this role), which governs connections to the universal higher consciousness. As such, violet is used in workings related to spiritual development and connecting to one's higher self, as well as developing and strengthening psychic ability. All aspects of occult wisdom are applicable here, including divination, meditation, magic, astral travel, dream recall, and other forms of mysticism.

As a color of spiritual healing and development, violet is used in workings related to psychic protection and restoring balance to empaths and other energetically sensitive people. Violet also promotes nurturing qualities, humility, forgiveness, and devotion to a person or a cause. In some traditions, violet is used to bring an end to bad luck. Violet is associated with the Element of Air, the planets Mercury, Saturn, and Jupiter, and the signs of Capricorn, Gemini, and Sagittarius. Its cardinal direction is East.

In this chapter, you'll find spells and rituals for communicating with the higher realms through the Element of Fire, increasing your capacity for joy, strengthening your devotion to an activity or cause, and transmuting negativity through spiritual alchemy.

ELEMENTAL FLAME COMMUNICATION

This exercise builds and strengthens your "psychic muscles" by directly interacting with the flame of your candle. You are actively connecting with the higher realms of consciousness—the domain of the color violet—in the form of the Element of Fire.

Note: For optimal results, you may want to spend a few days with the Indigo Zone Meditation Practice and/or the Indigo Psychic Receptivity Practice (above) before trying this one.

You will need:

- 1 violet pillar candle
- Journal or writing paper (optional)

Instructions:

Spend a few moments quieting your mind. When you are ready to begin, light the candle as you invoke the Element of Fire with the following (or similar) words:

"Element of Fire, thank you for the warmth and light you provide for all on Earth. I welcome your presence and your communication in this timeless moment. Blessed Be."

Gently train your gaze on the flame of the candle (be sure to blink when you need to).

Begin by simply watching the flame and taking mental note of its appearance. Is it still, or is it flickering rapidly? Is the flame rising high or leaning in any particular direction? Every candle is different, and every candle flame is a unique energetic presence in the Universe. Get acquainted with the spirit of this flame for a moment or two.

When you feel ready, begin trying to "shape" the flame with your own visualization of its appearance. With your eyes still open and trained on the flame, visualize it growing, shrinking, getting brighter and dimmer, leaning in a particular direction, flickering, waving, etc.

Keep your focus trained on the flame and the change you're visualizing at the same time. See how in-sync you can get the actual flame to be with your projection. You will have more success with this over time, with regular practice.

Finally, let go of working to shape the flame, and simply observe it again. Let your focus go very soft, and watch for images taking shape within the flame.

What do you see? What impressions or messages seem to be coming through? Spend a few moments in this receptive mode, without trying to analyze what you see.

When you feel finished, with the candle still burning, try spending 10 to 15 minutes freewriting in your journal about your experience. How did the flame respond to your visualizations of its size, direction, etc.? What images or other sensory data came through during the exercise?

After working this ritual a few times, reread your freewriting from each session and take note of any patterns that come up.

JOYFUL CROWN CHAKRA CONNECTION SPELL

This spell is designed to help you connect with the higher vibrational frequencies that allow you to attract more joy into your life. You are taking the feelings of joy that you experience in your heart center and pulling them up through your chakra system into the crown, where you can then experience a deeper connection with Universal higher consciousness. For it is in the deep feeling of joy that we know we are where we are meant to be!

Displaying the lists of joyful elements in your life helps to seal the energetic benefits of the spell. You may wish to keep them on your altar, place them on a vision board, or leave them somewhere else where you will see them often.

You will need:

- 3 violet candles
- 3 pieces of paper
- Violet marker or pen

Instructions:

On your altar or workspace, set up the three candles and place one piece of paper in front of each. Spend some time quieting your mind.

When you feel ready, light the first candle. Now take the paper in front of it and write down the names of all of the people that bring joy into your life. (You can use both sides of the paper if need be!)

Light the second candle and write down all of the places that make you feel joyful. These can be as simple as a sunny window in your home or as grand as the ocean.

Light the third candle and write down all of the experiences that bring joy into your life. These can be memories, but should also include recurring experiences that you still have access to.

If you wish, you can use additional sheets of paper to freewrite in more detail about these experiences, or you can just jot them down in note form.

When you are finished writing, gather all three of your lists and read them aloud, taking turns among the three categories. For example, read a name or two from the first list, and then read a place or two, then an experience.

Once you have read aloud all of the items on all three lists, hold the papers in your hands and say the following (or similar) words of gratitude:

"My life is filled with wonderful people, beautiful places, and joyful experiences. Blessed Be."

Place the lists somewhere where they will be frequently visible to you.

You can leave the candles burning, or gently extinguish them and relight them when you want to summon up a feeling of joyful connection to the Universe.

DEVOTION REVITALIZATION SPELL

Most of us have had the experience of starting a new hobby or activity—such as learning to play an instrument, studying a foreign language, or joining a book club—only to find that a few weeks or months later, our enthusiasm for the activity or cause has waned. This is often accompanied by at least some level of guilt or self-shaming for not "sticking it out," which is never helpful!

The next time you find your momentum flagging around an extracurricular that you do actually enjoy, try this spell instead of getting down on yourself for losing steam. Devotion can be cultivated and revitalized with some simple energetic adjustments—as long as you truly desire it!

You will need:

- 1 violet pillar candle
- Lemon, cedarwood, cinnamon, and/or patchouli essential oil
- Work candle for atmosphere
- Crystal point, athame, or other ritual carving tool
- Journal or writing paper (optional)

Instructions:

Light the work candle and spend some time quieting your mind.

Find a symbol that represents the activity or cause you're focusing on. You can use something emblematic of the activity (a soccer ball, a book, etc.) or an abstract symbol, such as a rune or a pentacle, that represents the devotion you're seeking to revitalize. Carve this symbol into the front of the violet candle, and anoint the candle with the oil.

Spend a few moments visualizing the feeling you had when you first began engaging with this activity. Enjoy the sensation of the excitement, ambition, anticipation, etc. that drove you to move from just thinking about the activity to actually doing it.

Now, focus on what you still truly enjoy about the activity. Make a list, either on paper or mentally, of every detail about it that makes the pursuit of it worthwhile. (If you feel any negativity creeping into your thoughts, such as notions of failure or guilt, etc., let them go and return your focus to the positive aspects.)

Finally, visualize a goal you can work toward, such as a particular level of skill/ability in the activity, that will enhance your enjoyment of it.

When you've reached a place of feeling enthusiasm again and are ready to seal this energy, light the candle as you say the following (or similar) words:

*"I celebrate the joy that [name of activity] brings
and rekindle my devotion to that joy.
Blessed Be."*

Allow the candle to burn for at least several more minutes before gently extinguishing it. Whenever you'd like to quickly rejuvenate your passion for the activity again, relight the candle and recall your visualizations from the spell.

VIOLET FLAME TRANSMUTATION RITUAL

This spell borrows from the ancient teachings of the Violet Flame, an alchemical energy known to many different spiritual traditions. Through this visualization, you can call on the Violet Flame for assistance with any kind of change you wish to manifest in your life.

Here, the focus is on transmuting the negative energy of unwanted memories. If you find yourself dogged by thoughts or reminders of an old experience that triggers sadness, anger, regret, or shame, bring in the healing power of the Violet Flame to set you free from those energetic attachments and create positive new experiences in their place.

Be sure to spend some time in meditation, or another form of grounding and centering, before this ritual, and work in a quiet and comfortable place where you will not be disturbed.

<u>You will need:</u>

- 1 violet spell or taper candle
- Work candle for atmosphere (optional)

Instructions:

Light the work candle, if using. Light the violet candle and focus your attention on the flame for a few moments.

When you're ready, close your eyes, bring the flame into your mind's eye, and say the following (or similar) words:

"I ask the Universal presence of the Violet Flame to manifest within me now."

With your eyes still closed, see the bright fiery color of the candle flame turning into a luminescent violet, and watch as the violet flame grows to fill your entire body.

When your body is fully alight with the flame, spin the flame in a clockwise direction throughout your physical form.

Now state your intention for transmuting the unwanted, with the following (or similar) words:

"I transmute the energies of these memories that no longer serve me. They are consumed in the Violet Flame."

Now it's time to state your intentions for what the transmuted energy can become, with the following (or similar) words:

"I am now filled with the energies of happiness and joy, and free to make new memories."

Take a deep breath, and when you're ready, slowly open your eyes. Take a moment to acknowledge the transmutation that has taken place, and the spiritual presence that assisted you. You can simply say something like:

"Thanks be to the Violet Flame for this change."

You can leave the candle burning, or gently extinguish it to use again for another Violet Flame ritual.

WHITE

As the sum total of all colors in the spectrum of visible light, white has long been associated with the qualities of unity, wholeness, truth, and peace. White represents the highest level of consciousness available to living beings. It symbolizes the "blank slate," the point of infinite potentiality for new creation within every moment. Perhaps this is why a white candle can be used in substitution for any other color when used in candle magic.

As a highly spiritual color, white is used in magical workings related to enlightenment, initiations, connecting to one's higher self, accessing the Akashic records, and other paths to spiritual growth. It is often associated with the crown chakra, which governs connection to the universal higher consciousness (although in some systems, violet plays this role).

White's purifying energies are used for cleansing and consecrating ritual tools and spaces, but can also be used to clear up confusion around complex situations. White is also used in magic related to inspiration and healing, new beginnings, completions, and balance, especially of one's personal energy.

White brings clarity to the cluttered mind, and aids with social anxiety, helping people to feel more comfortable and even extroverted around others. It is also associated with safety, making it great for protection workings. Its peaceful, unity-promoting properties make it ideal for workings related to conflict resolution, whether between individuals or groups of people, and for fresh starts after arguments or other troubles.

White has feminine energy and is often used to represent the Goddess in ritual. It is associated with the Moon and the sign of Pisces, as well as the Element of Air, making East its cardinal direction. However, white is also the color of the Fifth Element, also known as Akasha or Spirit. In this sense, white has no cardinal direction, but is instead associated with all directions.

You can use a white candle in place of any other candle in any spell in this book. This can be very handy when you have a particular magical need but no time to go out and buy the color that the spell calls for.

For an extra magical boost in this scenario, try also including crystals, ribbons, an altar cloth, or other objects that do visually represent the color you're actually working with. For example, if using a white candle in place of violet, add an amethyst or two to your altar or work space for the duration of the spell.

In this chapter, you'll find spells to bring clarity and new perspective to a situation, purify ritual and magical tools, work for peace in the world, and strengthen your physical body with the energy of white light.

"SPINNING WHEELS" CLARITY SPELL

When you're dealing with a problem that seems to refuse all possible solutions, it can be easy to keep spinning the same thoughts about it over and over in your mind. The fact is, you'll never come to a solution when you're still focused on the problem—you have to remove yourself from the vibrational frequency of the problem first.

This is easier said than done, of course, but with a sufficiently open mind, the following spell can get you there. The combination of white candle magic, quartz crystals, and the willingness to allow your subconscious mind to create new pathways to understanding the problem will help you get out of the "mud" in your mind and into a space where you can see things clearly again. This spell is ideally worked at night, shortly before going to bed.

You will need:

- 1 white pillar or taper candle
- 3 or more small quartz crystals
- Vetiver, peppermint, or clary sage essential oil
- Journal or writing paper

Instructions:

Anoint the candle with the oil. Place the quartz crystals around the candle in a circle (if using three stones, create a triangle, with one of the points nearest you). Take a few moments to quiet your mind.

When you're ready, light the candle, and begin to write.

You can start by identifying the problem, and then freewrite about how you're feeling about it at this moment.

Then write about how you will feel when the problem is solved—not how you will solve it, but simply what it will feel like when this particular problem is behind you.

Continue to write whatever comes to mind, without trying to direct yourself to a solution.

You may soon find yourself changing the subject altogether—if so, go with it! You are allowing your subconscious mind to merge with the vibrational frequencies of the candle and the quartz.

Continue to freewrite for at least 15 minutes, if not longer, until you feel a peaceful sense of detachment from the original topic.

When you're finished, gently extinguish the candle. Place one of the quartz crystals under your pillow before going to sleep, and pay attention to anything your dreams have to tell you.

Depending on your circumstances, you may wish to repeat the spell another time or two until you have the clarity you need to find your solution.

MAGICAL TOOLS CLEANSING RITUAL

Here's a simple, effective method for clearing out old energy from tools you use regularly in ritual and magic, such as your wand, athame, chalice, magical jewelry, talismans or charms (provided they're fire-proof!).

You may wish to clear your tools once a year, or more often, depending on your personal practice.

<u>You will need:</u>

- 3 white taper or pillar candles
- Copal or sandalwood incense
- Ritual/magical tools to be cleansed

<u>Instructions:</u>

Line the candles up in a horizontal row, a few inches apart, on your altar or work space. Light the incense and the candles. Take a moment to quiet your mind.

When you're ready to begin, pick up the item you wish to cleanse. Pass it quickly through the flame of each candle, visualizing all unwanted energy being "burned up" in the fire of each flame.

Repeat this with each ritual/magical item that needs to be cleared. When you have finished, gently extinguish the candles. You can reuse the candles for another cleansing ritual in the future, or use them for atmosphere in other workings.

GLOBAL PEACE SPELL

The goal of world peace is a noble one indeed, but clearly this is beyond the powers of any individual Witch, or it would have been accomplished by now! Nonetheless, we know that collective energy focused in a specific way can create amazing changes.

If you wish, you can contribute *very* powerful personal energy toward the collective goal of universal peace. This delightful spell provides an avenue for you to send strength and light to people all around the world.

You will need:

- 1 white spell candle
- Map of the world

Instructions:

Take a few deep breaths, releasing any negative thoughts on each exhale. When you're ready, light the candle.

As you allow some of the wax to melt, summon the feeling of peace within yourself. How does it feel when all is well in your world, with no conflicts disturbing your circle of family and friends? Imagine this feeling extending from you and radiating out in all directions, until it covers the entire planet.

Once a fair amount of wax has melted, begin working with your map.

First, send white light to the entire Earth, both the land and the oceans, until the map is bathed in white light in your mind's eye.

Now, working with one continent at a time, visualize the people living in each area of the world, and imagine sending the white light of peace to them.

Place a drop of wax on each continent to seal in your well wishes for peace in that area. As you do so, say the following (or similar) words:

"Peace begins within
and flows outward in infinite waves.
I send peace to all who dwell here,
as they and I are One.
Blessed Be."

When you have finished, take a final deep breath and gently extinguish the candle. Place the map on your altar or bury it in the Earth to send peace throughout.

WHITE LIGHT HEALING SPELL

While modern medicine has indeed made unprecedented progress in helping us heal from severe accidents and illnesses of all sorts, today's doctors are still largely unaware of the powers of the mind-body connection when it comes to our own ability to heal ourselves.

This spell is not meant to replace needed medical care, but it can work wonders in helping the body restore itself to its natural state of well-being. Whether you're dealing with a minor illness or injury or a serious medical condition, try working with healing white light in conjunction with your current treatment. Never underestimate the power of your own personal energy to improve your health!

Meditative music adds an extra healing effect to this spell. If you don't have any recordings of soothing music or nature sounds, search for free streaming ambient music online—you'll find plenty to choose from.

<u>You will need:</u>

- 9 white tea lights or votive candles
- Ambient music (optional)

<u>Instructions:</u>

Turn on the meditation music, if desired.

Sit on the floor or in a chair in the center of the room. Place the candles around you in a circle and then take several deep breaths, focusing on each inhale and exhale, to quiet your mind and focus your attention on your body.

When you're ready, light the candles one at a time, beginning in the cardinal direction of East and moving in a clockwise direction.

Once all nine candles are lit, sit back in the middle of the circle.

Close your eyes and focus your attention back on your breath for three counts.

Visualize a white light beginning in your heart center and gently spreading throughout your body. See the light pulsing into each area of your body, one at a time—your core, your legs and feet, shoulders, arms, hands, throat, and crown of the head.

Now focus extra white light in the area of your body you are working to heal.

Continue to breathe deeply, and envision all unwanted energy flowing out and away from your body as the white light continues to pulse through you. Maintain this visualization, breathing deeply, for at least 15 minutes.

When you are finished, gently extinguish the candles. Repeat the ritual daily, using the same candles, until the candles are spent. Depending on your body's needs, you may want to continue this practice for an extended period of time.

BLACK

As the counterpart to white, the sum of all colors, black is the result of the absence of light, and is therefore technically the absence of color. However, we still experience the color black in the night sky, in materials deep within the earth, and in many plant and animal species.

It's fair to say that black has had a negative reputation over the centuries, often associated with unpleasant topics like death and evil. In the realm of magic, black has definitely been associated with harmful or manipulative workings. However, those who work in accordance with the tenet of "do no harm" know how to utilize the energies of black for a variety of positive purposes.

Black is widely used in protection magic, as its ability to repel negative energy is unparalleled on the color wheel. (Many people who wear a lot of black clothing are sensitive, empathic types who are actually shielding themselves from the energies of others, whether or not they realize it.)

Black candles can be used in workings related to deflecting psychic attack, undoing negative workings, and banishing and/or binding negative influences. However, if you're dealing with other people in an emotionally charged situation, you may want to first consider other magical solutions, as black can be incredibly powerful in this context and may bring unintended consequences.

Black is excellent for increasing or reinforcing personal power (which, along with its protective properties, may be why Witches like to wear it so much!) and promoting independence. It is also the color of endings and release, making it ideal for workings related to ending unwanted habits, marking the end of a particular phase in life, dissolving obstacles, and getting out of relationships, jobs, or other unwanted circumstances.

It aids with transitions and transformations, lending stability to help one stay grounded and focused in the midst of upheaval. A color of hidden knowledge, black is useful for workings related to both keeping and discovering secrets, as well as divination techniques such as scrying or reading tea leaves.

Black is associated with the planet Saturn as well as the dark phase of the Moon. Its Elemental associations are Air and Earth, and its cardinal directions are East and North.

In the spells below, you'll work with black to banish negativity from yourself and from your home, shield yourself from external negativity, and activate a personal transformation.

CRYSTALLINE PROTECTION SHIELD

As you travel through your day, you encounter a multitude of energies—from other people, from situations, even from the vibrational echoes of events that occurred in a specific place. Much of this energy is positive, or at least neutral, but negative energy can be an unnecessary obstacle to feeling the way you want to feel.

The shielding qualities of black, combined with the talismanic properties of protective crystals, come together in this spell to help you create a vibrational shield of protection from any unwanted energies you may come across. This spell is particularly excellent for empaths, but is also useful for anyone who deals with a lot of different people and/or places in their daily life.

You will need:

- 1 black candle
- Cinnamon, clove, juniper, vetiver, or ylang ylang essential oil
- 1 piece of jade, jet, black tourmaline, or other protective crystal

Instructions:

Take a moment to breathe, relax, and release any stress you are feeling.

When you are ready, anoint the candle with the oil, light it, and place it in front of you. Pick up the protective crystal and hold it between your palms.

Now close your eyes and visualize the light emanating from the candle creating a protective shield around you.

See it start small and grow larger to encompass your entire body. Feel the light making a shield around you to protect you from any external negativity or ill will. Hold the light shield in your mind and strengthen its powers.

When you are ready, open your eyes, gently extinguish the candle, and know that you have created your own personal protection layer of light and love to carry with you through your daily life.

Carry the crystal with you in your pocket or purse as an added reminder to "activate" the protective shield.

You can repeat this spell any time you feel you need a renewed boost of protection against any unwanted energetic influences.

PERSONAL NEGATIVITY BANISHING SPELL

The first spell in this chapter is about protection from external negative energy—that which comes from influences outside of ourselves. When it comes to our *own* personal negative energy (and we all have some, at one point or another!), then a different approach is needed.

Magically, black is the color of banishing. A banishing, being the opposite of a summoning, is used to utterly un-invite something from your life. No life is completely without difficulty, and when something unwanted happens to us, a bit of negative energy from the experience often stays with us. This negative energy build-up can be seen as layers of dust upon our psyche.

This spell is a powerful banishing you can use as often as needed to give your spirit a good dusting off, and clear the way to healing, less stress, and the ability to truly move past difficulties.

You will need:

- 1 black candle
- 1 work candle for atmosphere
- Small slips of paper
- Fire-proof dish
- Journal or writing paper (optional)

Instructions:

Light the atmosphere candle and take a few moments to ground and center yourself.

When you're ready, begin writing in your journal about whatever it is that has caused you to want to work this spell, whether it's a current problem, an old memory, a feeling of generalized anxiety, etc.

As you write, know that you are emptying the negative energy from your physical body onto the page.

When you feel you have written enough, choose a few words or phrases that encapsulate the negative topics you have just written about. Write these on the small slips of paper. (You may only need one slip of paper for this, or you may want several—this is entirely up to you.)

Now light the black candle.

Take the first slip of paper and hold it over the candle flame until it ignites, then drop it into the dish to continue burning out on its own.

As you do so, say, *"I fully release the energy of _____."* Repeat this process for the remaining slips of paper.

When you are done, gently extinguish the candle.

For the next few days, you may wish to note any significant dreams or shifts in energy that occur and write them down in your journal.

FIRE-AND-WATER
HOUSE CLEANSING SPELL

The Blue Perimeter Home Protection spell, above, is great for keeping negative energy from entering your home. This spell, on the other hand, works to expel negative energy from *within* your dwelling space, and is quite handy for those living in old buildings.

This is an excellent spell to try when no amount of smudging (with sage, sweetgrass, or other powerful herbs) seems to quite get rid of all the less-than-pleasant energies in your home.

For best results, sweep or vacuum each room in the house before you begin, and close all windows.

You will need:

- 1 black floating candle
- Small bucket or cauldron

Instructions:

Fill the bucket or cauldron with water. Light the candle and float it on the surface of the water.

Beginning with the room(s) furthest from your front door, stand in the center of each room in your home.

Close your eyes and visualize all of the negative energy in the room being drawn to the flame of the candle. As it nears the cauldron or bucket, the energy is diverted by the flame into the water, where it is neutralized.

Once all of the negative energy has been drawn into the water, move to the next room, making your way toward the front door one room at a time.

When you are finished, stand near the front door and gently extinguish the candle.

Open the door and carry the bucket or cauldron outside. Take it all the way out to the street you live on (or the edge of your property), remove the candle, and pour the water out onto the Earth. Discard the candle in an outdoor trash can.

When you return to your home, open at least one window in each room, leaving it open for at least five minutes.

If you like, burn some sweetgrass or palo santo to enhance the energetic shifts now taking place.

TRANSFORMATION TALISMAN

Just as it takes an immense amount of pressure for the sand inside an oyster to transform into a pearl, personal transformation can be a slow and intense process. But, as any practitioner of magic learns, personal transformation is essential to a continually fulfilling life.

Whether you're working to lose weight, release an unwanted habit, regain independence after a breakup, or manifest any other daunting transformation, this spell will help you focus your positive intentions into a physical representation symbolizing this change. Enjoy the process of this spell, and then enjoy the enlivening process of transformation!

The shape of your talisman is up to you, but it should be fairly simple and represent the transformation you intend to achieve. Runes and other magical symbols can work well here, but you may also intuit your own original design. Just be aware that the more complex the symbol, the less sturdy it will be as a finished object.

You will need:

- 1 black taper candle
- Sand
- Bowl
- Journal or writing paper (optional)
- Small cloth bag (optional)

Instructions:

Place the sand in a bowl on your altar or table. Take a moment to relax and center yourself in your space.

Light the candle and set your intent of transformation. Spend some time conjuring up the feeling you want to have when you have accomplished your goal.

When you have a solid hold on this vision, draw your chosen symbol neatly in the sand, using your index finger.

When enough of the wax has melted, pour it into the design in the sand. You may have to allow extra time for more wax to melt to fill your shape. If so, continue to focus on your desired outcome. You may wish to journal about your goal during this time.

When you have filled the symbol with wax, place the bowl in the refrigerator or freezer for the wax to harden.

Once it has become solid, pop the wax shape out and clean any extra sand off of it.

Hold it in your hands and focus again on your transformational goal, and gently extinguish the candle.

You can keep your talisman on your altar to remind you of your goal, or carry it in a small cloth bag with you in your pocket, backpack, or purse.

SILVER

The feminine energy and enigmatic quality of the color silver has long linked it with the energy of the Moon, which is often said to cast a silvery light. Named for the precious metal that also bears this color, silver is a powerful, mysterious hue associated with all things psychic and divine.

As such, silver is often used in magical workings related to psychic awareness, whether it's clairvoyance, clairaudience, other forms of telepathy, or mediumship. Silver is good for strengthening intuition and divination skills and enhancing meditation, dream recall, and astral travel.

It is a color associated with wisdom and feminine power, and helps strengthen one's connection with the energies of the divine realms. It's also good for spellwork related to female fertility.

Silver's reflective properties can be used to help see into one's true self, which can help with navigating difficult or complex situations. It can also help with the frustrations often experienced when dealing with life's mysteries, by promoting patience and calm in the face of the unknown.

As a color with very fluid energies, silver helps one get better at "going with the flow" in quickly changing circumstances, and its similarity to the color grey makes it good for workings related to maintaining neutrality.

Silver is also used in spellwork for victory in endeavors involving luck, such as gambling, and is known to aid in attracting money quickly. It is a good color for workings related to intelligence and memory, particularly when thinking quickly is required, as well as stability, communication, and finding lost items.

Silver is a primary color of the Goddess and is used to represent her in Wiccan ritual, as well as for invoking or "drawing down" the Moon at Esbats. It is also associated with the signs of Gemini and Cancer, and the Element of Water. Its cardinal direction is West.

The spells in this chapter work with the energies of silver to reconnect with the divine feminine, connect psychically with the Element of Water, increase your gambling luck, and find lost items.

SILVER GODDESS-RECONNECTION SPELL

This spell is ideal for anyone who feels they have drifted from their spiritual path (which we all do from time to time). It's a lovely way to renew, to realign, and to reconnect with your personal relationship to the higher realms. It's a great spell for Wiccans in particular, but you don't actually have to worship the Goddess, or any goddess at all, to experience a deeper resonance with your own spiritual source.

Ultimately, this is about tapping into the essence of the divine feminine, which we all are a part of, no matter our individual beliefs. In the hustle and bustle of daily life, many of us are primarily engaged with masculine, or "yang" energy—the energy of "doing." Coming into greater balance means working with feminine, or "yin" energy as well, and learning to embrace "being."

You will be creating a magical talisman from a piece of jewelry with the vibrational frequencies of silver. You can use a favorite piece of silver jewelry or purchase a new one for this working. (Note: the jewelry doesn't have to be made of actual silver—a silver-colored piece will work fine.)

For an extra boost of the divine feminine energy, try this working on a New Moon or a Full Moon.

You will need:

- 3 silver spell candles
- 1 work candle for atmosphere (preferably white)
- Your favorite anointing oil (a single oil or a blend)
- Piece of silver jewelry

Instructions:

Light the work candle and arrange the three candles in a triangle on your altar or workspace. The base of the triangle should be facing you.

Anoint the jewelry with the oil, while focusing your intention on reconnecting with the divine feminine. Place the anointed jewelry in the center of the triangle.

Light the left base candle and say the following (or similar) words: *"I greet you, Goddess, at this new starting point along my path."*

Light the candle at the top of the triangle and say the following (or similar) words: *"I greet you, Mother Earth, every day that I walk upon you."*

Light the right base candle and say the following (or similar) words: *"I greet you, divine feminine, on all the days of my journey."*

To close the ritual, say the following (or similar) words:

"I thank you, Goddess, Mother Earth, divine feminine, for this time and place, this reconnection, and your eternal presence. Blessed Be."

Allow the candles to burn out on their own.

Wear the jewelry for ritual and magic, and/or in your everyday life.

TEMPERANCE WATER RITUAL

This soothing, meditative ritual is great for mulling over complicated issues, helping you to have the patience to allow things to work out in their own perfect timing. It's also great for simply calming the nerves, tapping into your psychic powers, and even getting into an ideal magical headspace prior to Esbats or any other ritual celebrations.

Here, you will be physically embodying the symbolism of the Temperance card, the 14th Major Arcana card of the Tarot. Virtually all Tarot decks feature the same basic image on this card: a figure, often female, who is pouring water back and forth between two vessels.

The symbolism is that of communication between the worlds, as well as of the need for balance and patience. The feminine energies and watery symbolism of the card makes it a perfect partner to the fluid vibrational frequencies of silver, combining in a ritual that promotes patience and calm, and welcomes psychic impressions, divine messages, and intuitive, non-verbal communication between your higher self and your subconscious mind.

If you don't have a Tarot deck, you can print an image of the Temperance card from any number of websites (or if you're artistically inclined, you can draw your own!). As for the dish ware, these items can be black, white, or silver colored (stainless steel is perfect).

You will need:

- 2 silver taper candles
- Large bowl or basin
- 2 cups
- Pitcher of water
- Temperance Tarot card (or image)
- Journal or writing paper (optional)

Instructions:

Place the bowl or basin between the two silver candles. Place the Temperance card where you can see it, but not so close to the water as to risk getting wet.

Light the candles and then pour the water very slowly from the pitcher into the bowl. If you like, speak some words about whatever dilemma (if any) you're working the spell in relation to, and ask for any advice or insight that may be available now.

Holding one cup in each hand, scoop and pour water from one cup to the other. Do this a few times, and then empty both cups back into the bowl and start again.

Continue to play with the water in this fashion as you feel yourself relaxing and your mind quieting.

Observe the water as it swirls around in the bowl, noting tiny details of bubbles, splashes and whirls as well as how the light bounces off of the water.

Allow any thoughts that come into the forefront to be noted and released, but don't try to "solve" anything—just softly play with the water. You may wish from time to time to gaze at the Temperance card, and see if any messages come through the imagery.

Continue to work with the water for at least 5 minutes, or until you feel a sense of serenity and completion take hold. If you wish, write down any thoughts or impressions related to the issue you spoke about when you first poured the water.

When you're finished with the ritual, gently extinguish the candles and pour the water outside on a tree or in the grass.

LUCKY-COIN GAMBLING SPELL

For those who enjoy the occasional trip to the casino or friendly poker game, here's a spell for a talisman to bring silver's lucky energy along.

Keep it hidden and secret, lest you allow any doubt to be introduced into your vibration. Good luck!

<u>You will need:</u>

- 1 silver spell candle
- Patchouli or cinnamon essential oil (optional)
- A silver coin (ideally a collector's item or foreign currency or something else you wouldn't spend)

<u>Instructions:</u>

Anoint the candle with the oil, if using. (You might also wish to anoint the coin.)

Place the coin in front of the candle.

Light the candle and as you allow some of the wax to melt, visualize having success at gambling.

Whether it's a card game, a slot machine, or any other game of chance, summon up the feeling of winning. See and feel the prize money in your hands.

Be as detailed with your visualization as possible, and stay focused on the vibrational frequency of the delight in winning.

When enough wax has melted, carefully tilt the candle to drip a drop of wax onto the "heads" side of the coin.

Replace the candle, and hold the coin several inches above the flame as you say the following (or similar) words:

"Lucky silver, lucky coin,
bring me luck and bring me gain.
Lucky money, lucky life,
I leave with more than when I came."

Place the coin in front of the candle and allow the candle to burn out on its own.

Bring your new talisman with you the next time you play games of chance.

LOST IS FOUND SPELL

Whether it's your keys, your phone, or something of less immediate importance, this spell can help you find your lost item.

Like any other magic, the most important aspect of this working is that you *believe* you will find what you have lost. If you keep your focus on the fact that you can't find it right this minute, then that will likely remain the case.

<u>You will need:</u>

- 2 silver candles
- 4-6 inch square of silver or black cloth

<u>Instructions:</u>

Place the cloth on your altar or work space, and place one candle on either side of it.

Light the candle to the left of the cloth, and state out loud what you are looking to find.

Now focus your attention on the cloth, and stare at it intently for at least 30 seconds.

Now close your eyes, and visualize the item you're seeking suddenly appearing, out of "nowhere," onto the cloth. See the item in as much detail as possible. Hold this vision steady for several moments.

When you feel ready, open your eyes and light the candle to the right of the cloth as you say the following (or similar) words:

"Lost is found, lost is found.
What I lost has just been found
and is on its way back to me.
It is done."

Fold up the cloth and place it somewhere on your altar, but in an inconspicuous place. You can tuck it under a crystal or candle, or simply place it off in a corner.

Gently extinguish the candles.

After the spell, trust that the item will come to you in perfect timing. When it does, you can shake out the cloth and return it to its regular place.

You can reuse the candles to repeat this spell for other lost items.

GOLD

Gold is the color of wheat fields, sunlight sparkling on water, and the precious metal that has been revered for thousands of years around the globe. A warm, optimistic, attractive color, gold holds the energy of the divine masculine, and the positive essence of aspiring to the highest standards.

Gold's properties make it excellent for magical workings related to success, achievement, confidence, courage, charm, and positive thinking. Its association with divine masculinity and with the mineral gold can be drawn upon for spellwork involving good fortune and abundance of all kinds, including financial wealth and prosperity.

Gold is even useful for manifesting luxury and extravagance, but it is more practically known for helping with better money management. Any matter involving happiness, blessings, or generosity is bound to benefit from the energies of this shining hue.

Gold also assists with connecting to the divine masculine in each person, regardless of gender. It can be used to boost inner strength, willpower, and intuition, and helps with the self-realization needed to heal emotional and psychic wounds from the past.

Workings related to any matter involving the need for justice, peace, and/or safety can benefit from the use of gold. This is a color of stability, which can be seen in the fact that the mineral gold, in its purest form, does not tarnish.

Gold is also useful in workings related to physical health, divination, and attracting good luck and money in a short amount of time. Some people also use gold candles during divination and for purification rituals.

Gold is a primary color of the God and is used to represent him on the Wiccan altar. It is associated with the Sun and with the Element of Fire, as well as the signs of Leo and Virgo. Its cardinal direction is South.

In the spells below, you'll work with the color gold to attract the energies of success, boost your ambition to achieve your goals, and increase your financial power, in the short and long term.

GOLDEN SCROLL SUCCESS SPELL

Whether you're facing a tough deadline, training to run a marathon, or taking on some other daunting task, the vibrations of the color gold can help you reach success in your endeavors.

This spell helps you to crystalize your focus on the alchemical blending of your own efforts with the support of the Universe. Use this spell for a boost of magical assistance from the higher realms any time you like!

You will need:

- 1 gold spell candle
- Bergamot, cinnamon, patchouli, ylang ylang, and/or lemon essential oil
- 1 or more work candles for atmosphere
- 1 piece goldstone or pyrite
- Slip of parchment or paper
- Several inches of gold thread
- Small cloth bag (optional)

Instructions:

Light the work candle(s). Anoint the gold spell candle with the oil.

Spend a few moments visualizing yourself succeeding at your goal. Imagine the feelings of relief, joy, triumph—whatever is appropriate for your situation—that you will experience once the goal is met.

Now consider what is needed from your end of things in order to meet the goal. For example, if you want to run a marathon, then diligent training will be required. If you're aiming to find a new job, then obviously you'll need to check job listings and polish up your resume.

Identify three actions you can take to "meet the Universe halfway" in your quest for success. Write these actions on the slip of parchment or paper, roll the paper into a scroll, and tie the gold thread around it.

Hold it gently between your palms as you say the following (or similar) words:

> *"I draw the energies of success*
> *into and through my whole being.*
> *I accomplish whatever I turn my attention to.*
> *And so it is."*

Now set the scroll in front of candle, holding it in place with the goldstone or pyrite. Allow the candle to burn out on its own.

You can place the scroll on your altar or carry it with you in a small cloth bag to remind you of your goal until it is accomplished.

GOLD AMBITION SPELL

When you're working your way up the ladder of success, you can sometimes lose sight of the big picture. If you're biding your time waiting for a promotion at a current job, considering a new career altogether, or wanting to strike out on your own in the world of self-employment, the energetic frequency of gold can help you boost your ambition to make the most out of your work.

You can use any size candle for this spell. If you'd like to repeat the spell for a few successive nights, use a pillar or taper candle so you can relight it each time.

You will need:

- 1 gold candle
- Bergamot, cinnamon, clove, patchouli, and/or lemon essential oil
- Crystal point, athame, or other ritual carving tool

Instructions:

Carve a symbol of your magical goal into the candle. This can be a "V" for victory, the rune Sowilo for success, a dollar sign, or a symbol that represents the kind of work you do (or want to be doing).

Take a few moments to envision how you want to feel about your work—whatever that may be. What does a successful day look like for you? What aspects of your work life can you see yourself being excited about? Visualize yourself filled with the energy of ambition, enthusiasm, and the drive to succeed.

When you have a strong hold on these positive feelings, light the candle as you say the following (or similar) words:

"Golden fire, golden flame—
ambition is my passion.
All is well above and below,
I am energized for action."

Now spend a few moments gazing at the candle. Visualize your energy going into the flame as it pushes up towards the sky.

Release any self-doubt or other negative thoughts or emotions that may have been draining your enthusiasm recently, and trust that you will soon be feeling the fire of ambition for your pursuits. Leave the candle to burn as long as you'd like.

PILE-OF-MONEY
ABUNDANCE SPELL

Those who work consciously with the Law of Attraction know that *like attracts like*. The more we think about something, the more it shows up in our experience. The trick is to choose to focus positively rather than negatively. In other words, if we're focused on the *lack* of the thing we want, then we simply attract more *lack*.

All magic works via the Law of Attraction, but this spell enacts it in a very direct way, by creating a visual display of financial accumulation that can be used as a talisman to keep your thoughts about finances positive.

The denomination of coins you use isn't important, but for best results, use nine coins of the same or similar size. You may want to use nine pennies, as their copper color is close to the vibrational frequency of gold.

You will need:

- 1 gold candle
- Bergamot, cinnamon, and/or patchouli essential oil (optional)
- 9 same-sized coins
- Small cloth bag (optional)

Instructions:

Anoint the candle with the oil, if using.

Now light the candle, and as you allow some of the wax to melt, visualize yourself literally sitting or lying upon a gigantic pile of valuable gold coins.

Visualize the room entirely filled with gold coins, all of which are yours to do whatever you like with. (If you wish, you can include some paper money in your visualization—whatever you need to feel truly abundant in the most luxurious fashion possible.)

When enough wax has melted, place one coin on your altar or work space and drop a bead of wax on top of it.

Quickly place the next coin on top in order to "glue" them together. As you do this, visualize the room filling with even more gold coins (or paper dollars).

Repeat the process of dripping a bead of wax onto the coin and stacking another on top. Each time, visualize your finances expanding and increasing.

When all nine coins have been stacked on top of each other, hold the stack carefully in your hands and say the following (or similar) words:

> *"My growing wealth is represented here in my hands.*
> *As positive energy builds upon itself, my money expands."*

Place the "pile of money" on your altar, in your home office, or in the place where you conduct most of your financial business.

Each time you see it, quickly visualize the room filled with gold coins and express gratitude for the financial abundance in your life.

SEVEN-DAY MONEY MAGIC

This spell is great for anyone wanting to strengthen their money manifesting "muscles." While it may not bring you millions of dollars, if done properly it will definitely bring you confidence in your ability to work magic for tangible results.

The repetitive aspect of the spell—working it every night for a week—allows you to strengthen your visualization powers and take note of your results each day. To gain maximum benefit from the spell, keep a running journal of both the work and the results. You can even think of it as something like a science experiment, with cash rewards!

You will need:

- 1 gold pillar or taper candle
- Anointing oil (optional)
- Crystal point, athame, or other ritual carving tool
- Journal or writing paper

Instructions:

Notch a candle in seven sections by lightly carving complete circles around it.

Anoint the candle with the oil, if using.

Each night, for seven consecutive nights, burn a single section of the candle.

As the candle burns, focus your attention on the idea of discovering money in random ways as you go about your day.

This can be as simple as finding a penny on the ground, or more elaborate, like discovering a 20-dollar bill in a pair of pants you haven't worn in ages.

The specific scenario you envision doesn't matter—the point is to conjure up the feeling of surprise and delight that happens whenever we come up on money unexpectedly.

Hold on to this feeling for as long as you can. If you like, you can repeat the following (or similar) words as the candle burns:

> *"Money on the ground, money all around,*
> *look at all the money I have just now found!"*

After the candle has burned through its notch for the night, gently extinguish it, and record any impressions you may have had during the work.

At the end of the following day, record any results—even seemingly insignificant ones like finding a penny on the ground!

Then repeat the spell using the next notch on the candle. Follow this routine until the candle has burned through its last notch.

Be sure to look back through your notes to see all of your results. Do you see any patterns emerge? Any correlations between your personal energy during your nighttime visualizations and your results the following day? How can you apply what you've learned in this experiment to the rest of your magical practice?

BROWN

Next to green, brown is perhaps the earthiest of all colors. We see it in the soil, the bark of many trees, the fallen leaves at the end of autumn, and the mud that comes with spring.

Brown is also a color of the harvest, the time when we bring in the rewards of our summer labors and set up for a secure and abundant winter. For these reasons and more, brown is definitely a color of practicality—of being "down to Earth."

As such, brown is a highly effective color in magical workings related to plants, animals—wild and domestic, but especially companion animals and livestock—and anything else to do with Nature. This is a color of generosity, stability and security, especially as it relates to the home, and it is often used in house-blessing rituals. Brown is useful for material gain of all kinds, and is excellent for spellwork focused on food and food security. It is also a go-to color for assistance with financial crises.

Brown is also associated with friendships, and is used in magic relating to trust, honesty, sincerity, and loyalty between friends. Its grounding and centering properties make it useful for balancing intense emotions, providing emotional support, and promoting strength and endurance. It aids with making decisions from a practical standpoint rather than emotional attachments, and reigns in indecisiveness.

Brown's steady, practical energies can be harnessed to strengthen or solidify developments already underway, particularly if they relate to real estate or construction. It is very helpful for situations requiring concentration and focus, such as studying for exams, and for finding lost items.

Brown is associated with both the planet and the Element of Earth, as well as the signs of Scorpio and Capricorn. Its cardinal direction is North.

In the spells below, the properties of brown are harnessed to help you get a garden off to a magical start, foster concentration while working on a large project, find a companion animal to join you on your life's journey, and promote balance in all aspects of your life.

GARDEN SEED BLESSING SPELL

Whether you're planting a full-fledged garden or just growing some herbs in pots on your window sill, this spell will give your plants a boost as they grow from tiny seeds into vibrant flowers, herbs, and/or vegetables.

You can work the spell for one packet of seeds at a time, but it will work just as well for all of your season's seeds in one go. Happy planting!

You will need:

- 2 brown spell candles
- 1 work candle for atmosphere
- Seed packet(s)

Instructions:

Light the work candle.

Arrange the seed packets in a pleasing manner (e.g. in a triangle or circle if you have enough packets) on your altar or work space.

Place one spell candle to either side of the seeds.

Light the spell candle to the left of the seeds.

Visualize the seeds beginning to stir under the surface of the soil. Watch as the first green shoots begin to reach for the surface and emerge into the open air. See the shoots continue to grow, pulsing with life force energy, as they allow themselves to be nourished by sunlight and water, until they are fully mature plants.

Visualize yourself enjoying your plants, whether through harvesting their nourishment or simply appreciating their beauty.

When you have reached this stage of the visualization, light the candle to the right of the seeds as you say the following (or similar) words:

"As above, so below,
I watch joyfully as you grow.
As below, so above,
these seeds are blessed with divine love."

Allow the candles to burn out on their own, and then plant your seeds.

FOCUS AND CONCENTRATION SPELL

Being fully focused is an enjoyable and fulfilling experience. Whether you're working on a school project, a hobby you're passionate about, or even a presentation for work, there's nothing better than losing yourself in the task—without distractions, without resistance, without even an awareness of time.

This simple spell draws on brown's vibrational frequencies to keep you focused and "in the zone" until the project is successfully completed. You may even finish the job in less time than you thought it would take!

For best results, work this spell at your desk or other work space, rather than your altar, since you'll want the candle burning near you as you work on your task.

You will need:

- 1 brown taper or pillar candle
- Ylang ylang, peppermint, or lemon essential oil

Instructions:

Anoint the candle with the oil, and spend a few moments quieting your mind.

Visualize the zone of focus you wish to experience through your task today.

When you're ready, take a deep breath and light the candle.

Now get to work, trusting that the Universe will bring you the focused energy you need to manifest your intention.

When you have completed the project (or the time you have to spend on the project), extinguish the candle.

Re-light the candle to re-enter the "zone" the next time you work on the project, or any time you need an extra boost of focus.

SPELL FOR FINDING YOUR COMPANION ANIMAL

While many people may think of their dogs and cats as "pets," those in the Witching world understand that a better term is "companion animal," since these animals are sentient beings in their own right. If you are planning to bring a companion animal into your life, it would be ideal to consider adopting from a shelter, since there are so many animals in need of loving homes.

The following spell can help you find the guidance you need for choosing your companion animal—or for being in the right place at the right time for your companion to choose you!

You will need:

- 1 brown spell candle or tea light
- Juniper, lavender, palmarosa, rose, and/or vetiver essential oil (optional)
- Crystal point, athame, or other ritual carving tool

Instructions:

Spend several minutes quieting your mind, through deep breathing, meditation, listening to calming music, or all of the above. The objective is to get into a space where you will be able to receive messages and impulses from the spiritual realm.

When you feel centered, carve a heart shape (or other symbol that represents love for you) into the candle. Then, anoint the candle with the oil, if using.

Now spend a few moments visualizing how you will feel when you have your companion animal beside you.

Feel the warmth of the animal beside you (or in your lap). Feel the soft fur/hair of the animal in your hand.

As you sink into this visualization, take note of any specific impressions that arise, such as the animal's size, color, sounds, textures, even possible names. (Don't worry if nothing specific comes to mind—just take note if it does.) Summon the feeling of joyful, unconditional love between you and your companion animal.

When you feel ready, light the candle and say the following words:

"I am ready to greet you, my loving friend. Thank you for sharing your life with me."

Allow the candle to burn all the way down, and have confidence that you will know your new companion as soon as you see her/him.

BALANCE AND STABILITY SPELL

Witches who raise energy as part of their ritual practice understand the importance of "Earthing," or grounding excess energy once the magical work has been completed. It's not only in ritual, however, that we can end up with more energy—whether it feels positive or negative— than is ideal for us to live balanced, stable lives.

This simple yet elegant spell uses the grounding energies of brown, as well as the literal Earth, to help draw out excess energy and rebalance body and mind. Try this anytime you feel out of sorts, or make it a regular practice—remember that the Earth is always good for you!

Ideally, this spell is worked outdoors on grass, sand, or some other flat area in Nature. If this isn't possible, then gather some soil from an outdoor area to use inside.

You will need:

- 4 brown tea lights or votive candles
- Outdoor area or pot of soil from the Earth

Instructions:

Find a quiet space outside and place the candles one in each cardinal direction (North, East, South, West), with enough room for you to fit inside the circle. Light each candle, starting in the North and moving clockwise.

When the candles are lit, sit in the middle of the circle. Place your hands directly on the earth and focus on releasing any negative energy while absorbing positive energy. Feel your body balance as the exchange of energy takes place.

Sit in this position for at least 5 minutes, but try to stay for longer, up to 30 minutes. When you feel grounded and balanced, thank the Earth for her healing energies and gently extinguish the candles.

GREY

The color of cloudy skies and rainy days, grey is often perceived to be a gloomy color. However, it can also be a welcome counterbalance against too much fiery energy from a long stretch of hot, sunny weather. The ultimate color of neutrality, grey helps us to take a step back, cool off a bit, slow down, and go inward. Grey is also the color of stone, and its energies are likewise solid, stable, strong, enduring, and ancient.

As the midpoint between white and black, grey contains properties associated with each. It is useful for magic relating to psychic ability, dreams, and intuition, as well as protection from negativity and binding, removing, or neutralizing negative influences. Grey is the quintessential color of balance, and can help whenever matters arise that challenge one's sense of serenity and composure.

It helps one maintain a calm reserve and patience when dealing with unknown outcomes, and with endurance during difficult circumstances. Grey also helps with releasing attachments to people, situations, and outcomes, and can soothe loneliness.

Grey is also used by some in "glamour" magic, to appear more appealing to others in any number of ways. It can be used in order to be treated with more respect, or to become "invisible," meaning that people you don't want to interact with won't notice you. The only caveat in this type of magic is to focus on the energy you project outward, rather than trying to control what other people think.

Use grey in workings related to complex decisions and other situations that require impartiality, discernment, contemplation, and objective observation and analysis. It is particularly excellent for neutralizing volatile or fiery conflicts, and resolving any situations that require compromise.

Grey is associated with the Moon and with the signs of Virgo, Scorpio, Cancer, and Capricorn. Its Elemental association is Water and its cardinal direction is West.

In this chapter, you'll find spells to help you avoid interacting with grouchy people, neutralize negative influences in your life, resolve a conflict, and see your way through an important decision.

ANTI-GROUCH INVISIBILITY SPELL

We've all had the experience of starting off in a great mood, only to be brought down by the grumblings and complaints of other people we encounter during our day.

This isn't necessarily intentional on their part—often they subconsciously interpret our happy vibes as an invitation to vent, in hopes that they will feel better after talking to us. However, the result is usually the opposite, as we simply end up sinking down to their lower vibration, while they stay focused on their unhappiness.

This spell utilizes the "cloaking" powers of the color grey to make you "invisible" to those whose negativity might otherwise cause them to latch on to your light. While they may still physically see you, you won't appear to be someone they want to unload on, leaving you free to cultivate your happy mood unobstructed.

You will need:

- 1 grey spell candle
- Cedarwood, clove, juniper, or vetiver essential oil (optional)

Instructions:

Anoint the candle with the oil, if using.

Spend a few moments cultivating a feeling of appreciation and gratitude for all that is going well in your life.

State these positive elements out loud, and aim for a list of at least 20. (These can be specific or general. They can be very simple things that you've recently experienced, like a smile from a child on the street or a nice meal, or long-term things like good health or a safe place to live.)

Now light the candle and take a few deep breaths. Visualize yourself walking through your day.

As you approach the vicinity of someone in a bad mood, see a grey mist covering you from head to toe, so that the person merely steps past you without realizing you're there.

At the same time, know that people with higher vibrational frequencies can still see you, and even share their positive energy with you whenever you cross paths. Summon up the feeling of well-being that comes from spending quality time with positive people, and the freedom from draining conversations that don't serve you.

When you feel confidently cloaked from any unwanted interactions, say the following (or similar) words:

> *"Now you see me, now you don't.*
> *If you're happy, you'll see me,*
> *if you're not, you won't!"*

Gently extinguish the candle.

If you like, you can repeat this spell with the same candle until it is spent.

NEGATIVE INFLUENCE NEUTRALIZER

While magic can help you eliminate negative energy from your environment and even dodge interactions with negative people (such as the Anti-Grouch Invisibility Spell above), sometimes there are unpleasant situations and people you simply can't avoid.

However, you don't have to get bogged down in the negativity surrounding the person or situation. This spell helps you to neutralize that negative energy so that it doesn't influence your thoughts or mood.

It's important to keep your focus not on individual people or conflicts, but on neutralizing the feelings they activate in you that you wish to be free from.

This is the best way to "do no harm" and avoid unintended consequences from your magic. It's also the most efficient way to improve your own circumstances, as you will be both neutralizing the negative influences and raising your vibrational frequency at the same time, which will reduce your chances of attracting negativity in general.

Depending on the size of your heat-proof dish, you may want to keep a small amount of water on hand just to be on the safe side.

You will need:

- 1 grey candle
- Small slip(s) of paper
- Glass bowl or other heat-proof dish
- Small cup of water (optional)

Instructions:

Light the candle as you say the following (or similar) words:

"I welcome transformational energy of the fire and now neutralize the following negative influences. So let it be."

On a slip of paper, write a single influence that you would like to banish. For example, you might write "the negativity surrounding this interpersonal conflict," or "the unease when I walk into my workplace," or "the feeling I get when someone complains to me."

Then fold the paper in half.

Carefully light the paper using the flame from the candle as you say the following (or similar) words:

"With harm to none, this energy is now returned to the Earth. It is done."

Place the burning paper in the glass dish.

As it continues to burn, visualize the negative influence being pulled out of your life and buried deep within the healing Earth.

Trust that the energy is now neutralized, clearing space within your vibrational field to attract more positivity into your life.

If you like, you can repeat this process with more negative influences, using more slips of paper.

When you are done, extinguish the candle. Take the ashes from the paper outside and bury them in the Earth.

CONFLICT RESOLUTION SPELL

Disagreements between two people are rarely completely cut and dry; often both people have salient points and good reasons for their thoughts and opinions about the subject at hand. With compassion and an open mind, it is always possible to come to a compromise that respects all parties involved. This spell can give you a big boost in that direction.

Note: before working this spell, make sure you have released any attachments to being "right," or to controlling the outcome in some way (such as needing the other person to "surrender" and agree with you completely). Otherwise, you risk being manipulative with your magical energy, which can easily backfire!

You will need:

- 1 grey spell candle
- Bergamot, lavender, palmarosa, rose, and/or ylang ylang essential oil
- Crystal point, athame, or other ritual carving tool

Instructions:

Take some time to ground and center.

When you're ready, carve your initials into one side of the candle.

Carve the initials of the person you're in conflict with into the other side, and then anoint the candle with the oil.

Spend a few moments focusing your attention on qualities you respect in the other person.

Make a mental list and strive for at least ten positive attributes about the person. If your thoughts wander to the argument or conflict, gently redirect them back into positive territory.

Now focus your attention on yourself. Make a mental list of at least ten aspects of yourself that you respect and are proud of. Note that some of these are likely to be on the other person's list as well.

When you feel a sense of peace and calm objectivity begin to take hold, light the candle as you say the following (or similar) words:

> *"Compassion, respect, and understanding bring peace.*
> *Let resolution come, and harmony reign.*
> *Blessed Be."*

Now release the conflict from your mind, trusting the Universe to respond to your focused intention with perfect timing.

Gently extinguish the candle, and know that the opportunity to resolve the conflict peacefully will soon present itself.

BIG DECISION BRANCH-OUT SPELL

When you've got a complex or monumental choice to make, especially one that seems cloudy or is causing you anxiety, grey is the optimal color for accessing a calm, neutral space from which to contemplate your options. This spell creates a magical brainstorming experience, in which you go beyond a "pros and cons" approach in a clear and focused way.

The tree here serves as a visual metaphor, so that you can view the range of possible outcomes all in one place. The branches represent the various pathways or outcomes that are likely to result from your possible choices. The trunk of the tree remains firmly in the ground, just as you will remain grounded as you consider the varied paths toward your future.

You will need:

- 1 large grey pillar candle
- Cinnamon, lavender, palmarosa, or peppermint essential oil (optional)
- Crystal point, athame, or other ritual carving tool
- Blank, unlined sheet of paper
- Journal or writing paper
- Grey pencil or marker

Instructions:

Spend a few moments quieting your mind. Don't think about your situation yet, but rather focus on your breathing and let go of extraneous thoughts.

On the front of the candle, carve an image of a large tree with many branches. As you create the tree, focus your intention on enjoying an anxiety-free time to peacefully ponder your next move, trusting your inner wisdom to come through in this time and place.

Then anoint the candle with the oil (if using).

Light the candle and with the pencil or marker draw a similar many-branched tree on the unlined paper.

For each possible choice involved in your decision, label a branch. For example, if you're trying to choose a new city to live in, name a branch for each place you're considering. If you're looking to solve a problem at work, label a branch for each possible solution you've thought of.

On another page in your journal, begin to write about the possible results of each choice. Don't be overly methodical about this—rather, start with whichever branch has the most energy for you in this moment. Freewrite about what you envision manifesting through this choice. Then move on to the next branch that you feel drawn to contemplate.

You may or may not arrive at a definitive answer by the end of this session, but you will have a clearer sense of where you're headed and much less anxiety about the question. Some decisions may take several days to work through, and new information or circumstances may shift your perspective on the matter. If so, you can always repeat the spell, with the same candle or a new one.

PINK

Pink is a quintessential color of love, with the fiery, passionate energies of red tempered by the higher vibrations of white. Seen in many types of flowers and blossoms, as well as in the sky at sunrise and sunset, pink exudes a cheerful, gentle, feminine energy that can be harnessed for many magical purposes relating to positive emotions and well-being.

Pink is the ideal candle color for all matters related to love, whether it's romantic, familial, the love between friends, or the ever-important love of self. It is associated with romance, passion, and sensuality, but its energies also encompass affection, kindness, compassion, and honor. Use pink in workings related to any situation that calls for the care and nurturing of others, and in any situation where you're finding it difficult to "do the right thing."

Pink's peaceful energies make it excellent for magic focused on friendship, companionship, and partnerships of all kinds. It is useful for manifesting and maintaining harmony—especially harmony within the home and within one's self. This includes spellwork related to forgiveness and reconciliation, and to spiritual and emotional healing.

For those who truly resonate with this color, it can be the ultimate aid in raising one's vibrational frequency, and can also assist with increasing physical energy. As a color of new beginnings, pink can contribute to success in all kinds of self-improvement endeavors.

Although it has been considered a color for "girls" since the mid-20th century, pink is actually associated with children and babies in general, and can be used in spellwork related to their health and protection, as well as workings for children to participate in. Pink is excellent for manifesting calm and relaxation, particularly when approaching a potentially frightening experience such as surgery.

Pink is associated with the planet Venus and the sign of Aries. Its Elemental association is Fire and its cardinal direction is South.

In this chapter, pink is used in a delightful spell to be worked with children, a spell to strengthen friendship, a magical romance recipe, and a ritual for strengthening self-love.

A SPELL FOR CHILDREN TO START THE DAY

Here's a spell you can teach your children to give their day a magical boost. It's great to do after breakfast and before everyone leaves for work and school, but you may want to first try it on a weekend morning, when time is more flexible. You can tell the children you're going to teach them a magic spell to make the day extra special.

All you need are a candle, pink chalk, and a patch of sidewalk or other concrete area to draw on. Depending on the age of the children, you may want to use an LED candle in lieu of actual flame.

<u>You will need:</u>

- 1 pink pillar candle
- Pink sidewalk chalk
- Sidewalk or other suitable concrete area

<u>Instructions:</u>

Begin by standing in a circle, with about two feet of space between each person.

Have each child trace their footprints on the ground with the chalk. Trace your own, too, if you like!

If there are only 2 or 3 people working the spell, then have each child trace their footprints twice to make a circle at least 4 feet in diameter.

When the chalk footprint circle is completed, place the candle in the center. Now pick a starting point on the circle facing East (the direction of beginnings).

Instruct the children to jump from one set of footprints to the next. As they jump they should shout out the following (or similar) words:

"Good fun, great day!
Magic powers light the way!"

Have them stop at each footprint and say one thing they want to go well that day, whether it's a test at school, having fun during playground time, getting along with friends, or enjoying the movie you're going to see.

When everyone (yourself included!) has jumped around the circle and spoken their intentions for the day, have each person return to standing in their drawn footprints, facing the candle in the center.

Carefully light the candle and then have everyone hold hands and repeat the spell words three times in unison.

Allow the children to gently blow out the candle. You can reuse the candle anytime you want to repeat the spell.

At the end of the day, ask the children what their favorite moments of the day were, and look for connections between their stated intentions that morning and the manifestations that unfolded over the course of the day.

FRIENDSHIP-STRENGTHENING SPELL

Sometimes even the best of friends can end up on the outs for no clear reason.

Whether you're dealing with communication difficulties, tensions from unknown causes, or a flat-out rift, this spell can help repair the strains that sometimes arise among friends. Drawing specifically on the combined vibrations of red and white, the spell seeks to temper passion with peace as you celebrate the strengths of both yourself and your friend.

Note: as with any spell involving another person, be sure your focus is on the desired outcome, rather than on magically manipulating another person's behavior. Otherwise, you run the risk of making the situation even worse!

You will need:

- 2 pink votives or tea lights
- Work candle for atmosphere
- Small amount of red and white paints
- 1 paint brush
- 5-inch square of pink poster board or card stock

Instructions:

Light the work candle and arrange the rest of the spell ingredients on your altar or work space.

Place the poster board or card stock in the center and then place one pink candle to either side of it, leaving enough space for you to work with the paints and brush.

Light the candle to the left of the poster board as you say the following (or similar) words:

"Let the light and love of friendship
shine throughout this work.
So let it be."

Using the white paint, paint a heart (or some other symbol of your friendship) onto the poster board.

Then, without rinsing the brush, swirl red paint into the white shape, to create the color pink.

While you swirl the red and white paint together, visualize a reconciliation with your friend. See the two of you laughing and having a good time together, and allow yourself to feel the way you do when you're enjoying time with this friend.

When the heart (or other shape) is completely pink, set down the paintbrush and light the candle to the right of the poster board as you say the following (or similar) words:

"The light and love of friendship
seals this working and strengthens our bond.
So let it be."

Allow the candles to burn while the paint dries. Then gently extinguish them and place the painting on your altar or in another specially designated location.

Trust that the opportunity to strengthen or repair the friendship will arrive in perfect timing.

STRAWBERRY SALAD
ROMANCE SPELL

This fun bit of kitchen witchery utilizes the potent romantic vibrations of pink. It's designed to attract a new romance, but can also be used to spice up an existing one.

Just make sure your magical intent is on the romantic experiences you want to have, rather than on the specific behavior of another person—otherwise the spell is likely to backfire!

As you prepare this cheerful fruit salad, be sure to focus your intention into the individual ingredients, as well as the process itself. Give your magic a boost by playing some fun, romantic music, burning some special incense or essential oils, and any other atmospheric enhancement that will help you keep your focus on manifesting romance through the power of Earth's delicious blessings.

Feel free to tailor the recipe to your liking. You can add and/or remove ingredients, tweak the amounts called for, etc. For best results, however, strive to keep pink as the dominant color of the salad.

This recipe makes approximately two servings and will keep for two days tightly covered in the refrigerator.

You will need:

- 2 pink candles
- Work candle for atmosphere (preferably pink or red)
- 2 cups strawberries, halved
- 1 cup raspberries
- 1 cup watermelon, chopped into bite-sized pieces
- ½ cup blueberries and/or blackberries
- ½ cup cherries, pitted
- 1 and ½ tablespoons fresh mint or basil leaves, chopped
- 3 teaspoons fresh squeezed lemon juice
- 1 and ½ teaspoons maple syrup or honey

Instructions:

Light the work candle and begin rinsing and chopping the fresh ingredients. If you like, you can imagine that you're preparing this dish for your new romantic partner.

Place all of the fruit in a bowl and stir in the mint or basil leaves, continuing to focus on your romantic desires.

In a small bowl or ramekin, whisk together the lemon juice and maple syrup or honey.

Pour on top of the fruit salad and mix gently until all the fruit is evenly coated with the dressing.

Now light the pink candles and say the following or similar words:

> *"This sweet and bountiful food, so lovingly prepared,*
> *brings forth the abundant essence of new love in my life.*
> *So let it be."*

Sit down and enjoy your enchanted strawberry creation!

As you do, continue to visualize the experiences of romance that you're seeking. What kind of person are you looking for? What will you talk about, where will you go, and how will you feel when you're together?

Enjoy fantasizing about your upcoming romance until you're finished enjoying your salad.

Put away any leftovers and gently extinguish the candles. You can relight them when you're entertaining your new romantic partner in your home!

SEVEN-DAY SELF-LOVE SPELL

In modern Western culture, the idea of self-love is often confused with selfishness, egotistical behavior. But the truth is that without loving ourselves, we're setting ourselves up for unhealthy relationships with others, as well as a wide range of disappointments in life.

Cultivating the vibrational frequency of self-love is arguably the most powerful kind of magic there is. This spell won't instantly remove all your blocks to loving yourself, but it can get you well established on the path toward profound emotional and spiritual healing.

<u>You will need:</u>

- 1 pink seven-day candle
- Journal or writing paper
- Mirror

<u>Instructions:</u>

Spend several minutes in quiet meditation. You may want to try the Indigo Zone Meditation Practice, above, or another brief grounding and centering technique.

When you're ready, light the candle. Spend several minutes freewriting about the idea of self-love.

What feels difficult or even unwanted about this concept? What might be blocking you from embracing the idea of loving yourself? Do you feel you have to have achieved specific things in order to deserve it, like losing weight, getting all your homework done, or being extraordinarily talented at something?

What if you could love yourself no matter what you look like, no matter what you do or don't do on any given day? What do you imagine an experience of true self-love might feel like?

There are no correct answers here—simply write openly and honestly about your relationship with yourself, and what you would like to see develop from this point.

When you're finished writing, pick up the mirror and look your reflection in the eyes.

Say out loud, to yourself, "I love you," three times.

Don't worry if this feels silly or even unpleasant—these are normal reactions at first. Say the words anyway, being sure to look yourself in the eye.

(Note, if you don't have a portable mirror, you can do this step in front of any mounted mirror.)

Allow the candle to burn out on its own, which typically takes seven days. At least once each day, make a point of looking in the mirror and saying "I love you" to yourself, three times.

Every time you notice the candle, remind yourself that you are worth this magical work, just by virtue of being alive and being yourself.

Take note of any shifts in your emotional, spiritual, and even physical experiences during this period. Consider maintaining the mirror ritual for at least thirty days, and note how it gets easier over time.

CONCLUSION

As you explore and develop your practice of candle magic, you will be strengthening your relationship with the Element of Fire, and with the infinite possibilities contained within the vibrational frequencies of the visible light spectrum.

If you keep track of your spellwork in a Book of Shadows or a journal, you may discover over time that certain colors produce more powerful results for you than others. This may be because you prefer certain colors on an aesthetic level, or because elements of your personal vibrational frequency tend to resonate with those colors. Either way, it can be a delightful process to develop your own preferred magical "color palette," building on your prior experience with a few choice colors and expanding into related shades and hues.

However, don't focus too narrowly on a small handful of colors, or you may miss out on new magical discoveries. Branch out from time to time and try a spell with a color you don't automatically resonate with. You may be surprised at what new experiences these less familiar colors can bring into your life!

As a final reminder, feel free to use any of these spells as a template from which to design your own, and always follow the wisdom of your inner Witch. And no matter what, use caution—it is important to remember and respect the destructive capacities of Fire. Enjoy your journey with the magic of candles. Here's to a vibrant, multicolored, warm and illuminating magical life!

FREE AUDIOBOOK PROMOTION

Don't forget, you can now enjoy a free audiobook version of any of my books when you start a free 30-day trial with Audible. This includes best-sellers such as *Wicca for Beginners* and *Wicca Book of Spells*.

Members receive free audiobooks every month, as well as exclusive discounts. And, if you don't want to continue with Audible, just remember to cancel your membership. You won't be charged a cent, and you'll get to keep your book!

To download this or any of my 20+ books on Wicca and related topics, simply visit:

www.wiccaliving.com/free-audiobook

Happy listening!

MORE BOOKS BY
LISA CHAMBERLAIN

Wicca for Beginners: A Guide to Wiccan Beliefs, Rituals, Magic, and Witchcraft

Wicca Book of Spells: A Book of Shadows for Wiccans, Witches, and Other Practitioners of Magic

Wicca Herbal Magic: A Beginner's Guide to Practicing Wiccan Herbal Magic, with Simple Herb Spells

Wicca Book of Herbal Spells: A Book of Shadows for Wiccans, Witches, and Other Practitioners of Herbal Magic

Wicca Candle Magic: A Beginner's Guide to Practicing Wiccan Candle Magic, with Simple Candle Spells

Wicca Book of Candle Spells: A Book of Shadows for Wiccans, Witches, and Other Practitioners of Candle Magic

Wicca Crystal Magic: A Beginner's Guide to Practicing Wiccan Crystal Magic, with Simple Crystal Spells

Wicca Book of Crystal Spells: A Book of Shadows for Wiccans, Witches, and Other Practitioners of Crystal Magic

Tarot for Beginners: A Guide to Psychic Tarot Reading, Real Tarot Card Meanings, and Simple Tarot Spreads

Runes for Beginners: A Guide to Reading Runes in Divination, Rune Magic, and the Meaning of the Elder Futhark Runes

Wicca Moon Magic: A Wiccan's Guide and Grimoire for Working Magic with Lunar Energies

Wicca Wheel of the Year Magic: A Beginner's Guide to the Sabbats, with History, Symbolism, Celebration Ideas, and Dedicated Sabbat Spells

Wicca Kitchen Witchery: A Beginner's Guide to Magical Cooking, with Simple Spells and Recipes

Wicca Essential Oils Magic: A Beginner's Guide to Working with Magical Oils, with Simple Recipes and Spells

Wicca Elemental Magic: A Guide to the Elements, Witchcraft, and Magical Spells

Wicca Magical Deities: A Guide to the Wiccan God and Goddess, and Choosing a Deity to Work Magic With

Wicca Living a Magical Life: A Guide to Initiation and Navigating Your Journey in the Craft

Magic and the Law of Attraction: A Witch's Guide to the Magic of Intention, Raising Your Frequency, and Building Your Reality

Wicca Altar and Tools: A Beginner's Guide to Wiccan Altars, Tools for Spellwork, and Casting the Circle

Wicca Finding Your Path: A Beginner's Guide to Wiccan Traditions, Solitary Practitioners, Eclectic Witches, Covens, and Circles

Wicca Book of Shadows: A Beginner's Guide to Keeping Your Own Book of Shadows and the History of Grimoires

Modern Witchcraft and Magic for Beginners: A Guide to Traditional and Contemporary Paths, with Magical Techniques for the Beginner Witch

FREE GIFT REMINDER

As a thank-you gift to my readers, you can also download a free eBook version of *Wicca: Little Book of Spells.* These ten spells are ideal for newcomers to the practice of magic, but are also suitable for any level of experience!

You can download it by visiting:

www.wiccaliving.com/bonus

I hope you enjoy it!

DID YOU ENJOY
WICCA BOOK OF CANDLE SPELLS?

Thanks so much for reading this book! I know there are many great books out there about Wicca, so I really appreciate you choosing this one.

If you enjoyed the book, I have a small favor to ask—would you take a couple of minutes to leave a review for this book on Amazon?

Your feedback will help me to make improvements to this book, and to create even better ones in the future. It will also help me develop new ideas for books on other topics that might be of interest to you. Thanks in advance for your help!

Printed by Amazon Italia Logistica S.r.l.
Torrazza Piemonte (TO), Italy

12682928R00073